ACPL ITEM
DISCARDED

D1601339

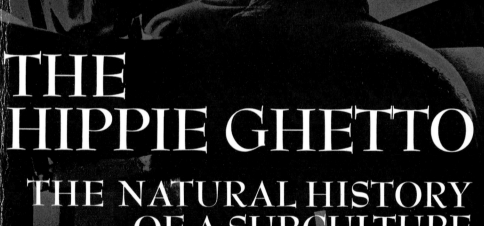

THE
HIPPIE GHETTO
THE NATURAL HISTORY
OF A SUBCULTURE

WILLIAM L. PARTRIDGE

CASE STUDIES IN

CULTURAL ANTHROPOLOGY

GENERAL EDITORS

George and Louise Spindler

STANFORD UNIVERSITY

THE HIPPIE GHETTO

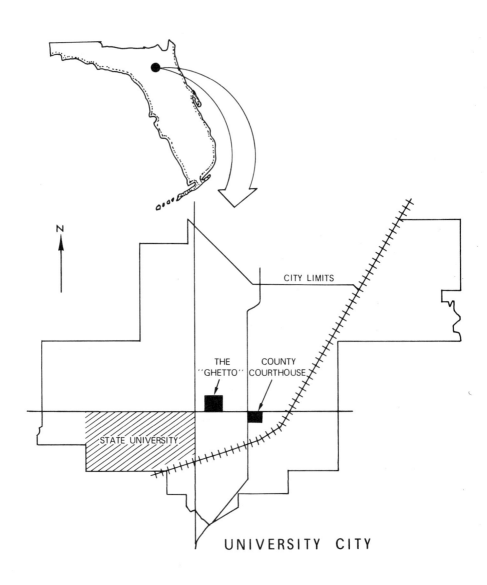

N

CITY LIMITS

THE
"GHETTO"

COUNTY
COURTHOUSE

STATE UNIVERSITY

UNIVERSITY CITY

THE HIPPIE GHETTO

The Natural History
of a Subculture

By

WILLIAM L. PARTRIDGE

University of Florida, Gainesville

HOLT, RINEHART AND WINSTON, INC.

NEW YORK   CHICAGO   SAN FRANCISCO   ATLANTA

DALLAS   MONTREAL   TORONTO   LONDON   SYDNEY

Copyright © 1973 by Holt, Rinehart and Winston, Inc.
Library of Congress Catalog Card Number: 72–84769
ISBN: 0–03–091081–1
Printed in the United States of America
3 4 5 6 7   059   9 8 7 6 5 4 3 2 1

Allegory for America

"For sweetest things turne sourest by their deedes,
Lillies that fester, smell far worse than weeds."

"For I have sworne thee faire, and thought thee bright,
Who art as black as hell, as darke as night."

From sonnets by Shakespeare, as it appeared on the cover of *The Great Speckled Bird,* designed and drawn by a resident of the University City hippie ghetto.

Foreword

About the Series

These case studies in cultural anthropology are designed to bring to students, in beginning and intermediate courses in the social sciences, insights into the richness and complexity of human life as it is lived in different ways and in different places. They are written by men and women who have lived in the societies they write about and who are professionally trained as observers and interpreters of human behavior. The authors are also teachers, and in writing their books they have kept the students who will read them foremost in their minds. It is our belief that when an understanding of ways of life very different from one's own is gained, abstractions and generalizations about social structure, cultural values, subsistence techniques, and the other universal categories of human social behavior become meaningful.

About the Author

The author is a doctoral candidate in anthropology at the University of Florida in Gainesville. The data from which this case study has been written were collected while he carried out field research for the Master of Arts degree during 1967 and 1968.

Mr. Partridge became interested in the "hippie movement" during 1966 when the national news media publicized the migration of young people to the Haight-Ashbury district of San Francisco. Being acquainted with such a population in the town he calls University City, Partridge moved into the neighborhood called the "ghetto" and became a participant in the culture of the people who lived there, distinguished from the other residents by the fact that he was an anthropological researcher who took notes on the social organization, beliefs, and activities of his fellow residents.

This case study was prepared while Partridge was Instructor of Social Sciences at the University of Florida. He has read several papers before professional societies in which he presented some of the data discussed in this case study. He has also published an article dealing with this community in the Southern Anthropological Society Proceedings (Partridge 1971).

At present the author is living on the north coast of Colombia, South America, where he is conducting research into the role of marijuana use in a traditional peasant community.

About the Book

This case study is an objective analysis by an anthropologist of the sub-culture of a hippie ghetto. William Partridge spent over a year as a participant-observer in the ghetto. He returned later to recheck his earlier observations.

Partridge chooses not to regard the hippie ghetto group as a counter-culture, as others have (Roszak 1968), since, he writes, it is in reality "a part of and a product of American society." Partridge believes, as does Anthony Wallace (1969), that the core hippie values are drawn from the cultural heritage of Western civilization and Judeo-Christian mythology. He draws an analogy between the Christian of Western mythology journeying to Mount Zion and the idealized personality of the hippie ghetto—a heroic individual (usually an "elder") "buffeted by the caprices of ignorant 'straights' but true to his inner, personal values."

Certain of these core values such as isolation, experimentation, intimacy, transience, and communal intoxication, the author explains, are expressions of inter-action patterns which have developed among hippies as they have attempted solutions to the problems of group life, sex, subsistence, housing, entertainment, and other conditions of existence.

The author asks: "What is a hippie?", and finds definition impossible, as there are many different kinds of hippies on the American scene. The "Hippie Culture" would consist of a conglomeration of Christian mysticism, Vedic teachings, revolutionary tracts, Madison Avenue pop-psychology, pseudo American Indian religions, hedonism, and some traditional American values, such as individualism, independence, and frontier courage. Each different group seizes upon certain elements of this set of choices to devote its energies to and to elaborate upon.

Partridge circumvents the problems of formal definition by describing and tracing in detail the process by which those who call themselves hippies arrive at a definition and identification as hippies. The focus is upon residents of a hippie ghetto in University City—a southern university town—who are or were students.

The reader can empathize with the new initiate, step by step, as he or she learns from the "elders" during the period of experimentation. The reader can, for example, vicariously participate in the important "rap session," a form of ritualized communication. The purpose of these frequently held sessions is the establishment of rapport among the group through members conversing openly and honestly with one another. The ritual involves smoking marijuana as the sharing of a "sacrament" considered necessary for communication. Since newspapers and media from the straight society are to be mistrusted, the emphasis in discussions is upon personal experience.

The last chapter is an attempt to relate the specific case materials and ethnographic detail in the study of the ghetto to the discipline of anthropology. The student interested in change and the proliferation of subcultures on the modern scene welcomes the discussion, in more general terms, of the hippie movement. Partridge utilizes concepts such as "rites of intensification" and "revitalization movements" as an integral part of the analysis.

We feel that this case study is of interest not only because it describes a notorious subculture with the objectivity of a social scientist, but also because it is a study of a subculture that both represents a transformative change sweeping American society and is also a partial cause of some of it. Dress styles, art, music, sexual mores, and the use of drugs have all been influenced in various degrees and ways by phenomena that can be broadly subsumed under the category "Hippie Culture." This subculture also calls to our attention, both as adults and as youth, the fact that our "straight" society is in need of transformative change. The distrust of the establishment and its institutions, even its media, is profound and thought-provoking.

GEORGE AND LOUISE SPINDLER
General Editors

Stanford, California

Preface

The young people, a segment of whose lives I describe in the pages that follow, can all too readily be labeled as exemplifying Theodore Roszak's idea of a "counter-culture."[1] This would be a distortion of both the facts and my purpose in examining their behavior and seeking an understanding of it. The "hippie movement" is not in dialectical opposition to American culture. Its adherents are offspring of middle-class white Americans, who were socialized in the American city, suburb, and school, drafted into the American armed forces, and who carry and transmit American behaviors, ideals, and myths. The group with which I lived for over a year is just as much a part and product of American society as are asylums, jails, and homes for the aged, violence, conflict, and rebellion.

Anthropological training teaches one to view society as a stream of activity—particular events appearing and disappearing with a certain rhythm—which is mediated by seasonal changes and culturally patterned world views. The individual human life cycle is seen as an expression of the rhythmic pattern of the life of a people, a pattern of life that finds its source not only in the actions of certain men, but in the actions of certain universal processes of nature. We are not concerned here with the individual phenomenon *qua* phenomenon but with its function as part of a cultural process. During times of tension or stress, however, we have a different perspective, and society looks quite different. At times like these society fractionates before our eyes as first one group and then another acts upon the problems its members feel to be acute. Periods of conflict act like a prism, refracting the constituent components of the whole. The decade of the 1960s was such a period, and the analogy is useful for stating the purpose of this case study. But there is a pitfall in the analogy. The danger is that one's vision may become blinded to the larger social and cultural whole of which conflict and tension are mere parts. As one seeks to define and describe the events and activities that shape the conflict, his vision may become myopic. Those who fall prey to this danger come to the conclusion that the phenomenon under study is unique; that it is different from social phenomena at other times and in other places. Even worse, the phenomenon under study often comes to be defined in terms of what it is not. Society is bifurcated into positive and negative elements, for and against, black and white. The spectrum of social life is lost in dialectics.

Polar concepts and their matching labels are such utilitarian, perhaps even necessary, parts of daily life in America that we find ourselves easy prey to their appeal in analytic writing. Dialectics economize the energy we might normally expend thinking, and they keep our minds free of the complex and complicated facts and qualifications which must accompany understanding. My purpose in the

[1] Theodore Roszak, *The Making of a Counter Culture*, New York: Anchor, 1968.

pages that follow is to examine the empirical evidence obtained during field research and not to defend one label or another.

The anthropologist studying American culture confronts special problems as he turns his analytical tools upon those who are friend and kin to him. These are not only of an ethical nature but are also of practical importance in carrying out the tasks of research and writing. As a member of American society he moves freely in areas that might be blocked if he were less familiar with the nuances of language and custom of a culture foreign to him. But he does not have the special, even "sacred," role of stranger in a land among a people he does not know. The researcher is allowed fewer mistakes, enjoys the privileges and sanctions of group life quite readily, and is expected in general to "know" what is proper and improper. When I became interested in the phenomenon labeled the "hippie movement" by the media, early in 1967, and had determined that I would attempt a participant–observer study of a neighborhood called the "ghetto" by students who lived there, I did not know what constituted proper and improper behavior of a ghetto resident. Through a friend in the ghetto I learned that an apartment was being vacated and I moved into it, hoping that I would soon be enlightened. As it turned out, my hopes were fulfilled.

The data were collected during the period from June 1967 to August 1968. Data collection and observation were done by the natural history method (Arensberg and Kimball 1965)[2] and the traditions of community studies in social anthropology, although the ghetto cannot actually be termed a community since only one generation of individuals lives there. Yet the natural history method was an important tool for I was concerned with recording the movement of ghetto residents through time and space, their customary patterns of interaction, the fluctuating levels of interaction intensity, the events that defined and gave meaning to their lives, and the conditions that provided the context of ghetto life. The residents of the ghetto either all had recently been or were at the time students at State University. They ranged in age from adolescent to young adult, came from white, middle-class background, and were of both sexes. The ghetto population which is described here, averaged from forty to fifty in 1967 and 1968, but it should be emphasized that the ghetto was rapidly expanding; by the time I had finished my study and left the ghetto I would estimate that the population had multiplied several times over and that many areas of town had sprouted hippie populations.

My role as researcher was ambiguous for several reasons. First, I was a student and had known many of the residents of the ghetto prior to the period of study. I identified myself as an anthropological researcher doing a study of the hippie ghetto. This created no obstacles until I encountered a network of drug dealers who handled and used heroin. After an initial invitation and my subsequent refusal to join this network I was seldom engaged in conversation by any of these persons. A few days after my refusal of the invitation (to buy heroin) I passed a known dealer and user on the street and he refused to speak. Not all heroin dealers were this distant, but I collected little data from them. This was unfortunate, but un-

[2] Conrad M. Arensberg and Solon T. Kimball, *Culture and Community*, New York: Harcourt Brace Jovanovich, 1965.

derstandable, since drug dealers are among the most mobile members of the ghetto and some of the most important vehicles of communication between hippie groups in different cities and towns. These communication networks are an important part of ghetto life and the lack of data represents a distressing void in this description. It will become evident that the effect of a high degree of mobility between hippie groups can be described, but a description of the functioning of these networks must be omitted. Access to other groups in the ghetto was never denied in this way and I readily became a participant–observer in all aspects of ghetto life.

In leaving the ghetto in September 1968 I ceased to play the role of full-time participant–observer. I became, during the year that followed, a part-time participant and part-time observer. But the data collected in 1967 and 1968 did not lie dormant, for my part-time relations with the ghetto population provided still other data that augmented and clarified my earlier data. It was mainly this part-time role that convinced me of the value of the natural history method of study and analysis for examining an ongoing social and cultural process. Had I written up my conclusions immediately after leaving the ghetto I probably would have produced a much more static model of social interaction. This is simply another way of saying that often more than a year of observation is needed for the anthropologist to understand the dynamics of the life-style of a group of people. The natural history method provides an important framework for interpreting the dynamics of social life through time and space. Some discussion of this particular intellectual tradition, the models used, and the manner of ordering data is necessary here.

The natural history method of study is built upon the organic model of a social system. Those who see the recent public interest in ecology as a new and refreshing development often forget that a few American anthropologists have been utilizing ecological concepts for well over half a century. Human society is one element in an elaborate system of relations between man and his environment. The natural history method of study in social science focuses our attention upon the relationships which obtain among elements in human society, much the same as a biologist is concerned with relationships among the parts of an individual organism or the ecologist is concerned with relationships among parts of an ecosystem such as a pond or forest. By focusing upon the relations among the parts of a system of human social life the anthropologist who uses the natural history method studies changes that occur through time and space. He observes the interactions between individuals, groups, or societies at Time 1 and then again at Time 2. He examines the way in which individuals, groups, and societies interact in Place A and then again in Place B. Through careful observation in this manner the observer is able to gather empirical data that reflect a process of change, that is, he is able to construct the natural history of social life.

An important aspect of the natural history method of study is the way in which an observer classifies the constituent elements of a social system. In the chapters that follow we will have the opportunity to consider classificatory labels that have been used by other social sciences such as the "alienated individual," the "anomic social system," and the "search for identity." Each of these as well as other taxa are often useful for organizing our thoughts, but they explain very little and provide little understanding of the process of social life. For example, it is obvious that the hippie can easily be classified as a deviant person, much the same way as sociologists have treated the hobo, the Bohemian, the alcoholic, the junkie, the homosexual, and the criminal (Clinard 1964).[3] But such flat statements, which usually seem pejorative, do not tell us anything about how deviates live, where they come from, and where they are going. Moreover, they tell us nothing of the deviates' relation to a larger social and cultural whole. We are left to speculate over the meaning of the word deviant. Likewise, those who say that students are alienated are utilizing an essentially trite label, valuable as taxa but not very informative.

By focusing attention on the significant events of the social life of hippie ghetto residents and observing changes in their patterns of interaction, the relationships in which they engage themselves, the activities in which they participate, and the rhythmic fluctuations which occur over time and space, it becomes possible to describe the hippie ghetto as an ongoing social process. Then one might still claim that the hippie is a deviant manifesting certain typological characteristics of deviant persons in general and one might still say that they are alienated from the larger society. But one will also be aware of the way in which this human grouping is related to the larger society, where it comes from, and where it is going. In short, deviancy and alienation can be seen as essentially dynamic in nature, as possessing a definite structure, and as part of a much larger cultural process.

The organic model of a social system is well articulated by Arensberg and Kimball.[4] These anthropologists state that an understanding of the processes of social and cultural life is not to be found in the minute genetic maps upon which individuals of a species are replicated, nor does it reside in the *élan vital* of certain kinds of organisms, nor is it to be found in the invisible "black box" of the individual psyche. Rather, an understanding of the process of social and cultural life is gained through examining the recurrent and regular structures of human social organization, the relations between parts of a system. Classificatory devices are needed, to be sure; one must distinguish between the parts of the system. But the authors are quick to point out that taxonomies are not to be developed *a priori*, but as they grow out of the data themselves.[5] The first five chapters are presented under headings that can be called elements or parts of the hippie ghetto social and cultural system: the place, the people, the relationships, the activities, and the values and sentiments. The final chapters, the process and the movement, are the author's interpretation of the nature of the ghetto social system. The organic model of a social system, then, can be broken down into component parts. But it must be recognized that such divisions are conceptualizations; in each we will find the elements of all the others and, hence, in each we will see reflections of the whole.

[3] Marshall B. Clinard, *Anomie and Deviant Behavior*, New York: The Free Press, 1964, p. 24.
[4] *Ibid.*
[5] *Ibid.*, p. 31.

Acknowledgments

An honest listing of those who have contributed to my efforts to sharpen and clarify my data would stretch many pages. But there are some whose ideas, suggestions, and teachings have been compelling, so much so that at times it becomes difficult to give them proper mention since their ideas have become part of my own. Among these is Professor Solon T. Kimball, whose intellectual interests and activities provided a vigorous source of theoretical stimulation. It was through his classes and seminars that I was exposed to the natural history method of social anthropology, the framework in which the work was carried out and in which it is presented here. He also read the completed manuscript, asking questions and offering criticisms which at times provoked the rewriting of entire chapters. For this interest in the work of one of his students Dr. Kimball deserves a large measure of recognition for any merit that may be found in this book.

Those of the faculty of anthropology who have contributed directly to the writer's work by offering suggestions and by reading portions of the manuscript are Professors Sarah A. Robinson (Assistant Professor, 1963–1968), who provided guidance and training in some of the basic techniques of data collection utilized; Brian M. duToit, Theron A. Nunez, and G. Alexander Moore, who each read portions of an earlier draft and offered valuable comments of a theoretical, comparative, and interpretive nature.

Portions of the manuscript have appeared as an article published by the Southern Anthropological Society.[6] Special thanks go to Dr. J. Kenneth Morland, volume editor, and Dr. Charles Hudson, editor of the society's *Proceedings*, for their interest in and promotion of studies of contemporary cultures and societies in the south. Both Dr. Morland and Dr. Hudson provided constructive criticisms of that article, many of which have been incorporated here.

For financial assistance while pursuing my course of training in anthropology I am indebted to Dr. Charles H. Fairbanks, who provided employment as a graduate assistant in the Department of Anthropology and to Dr. Herbert J. Doherty, who provided employment as a teaching assistant and later as an instructor in the Social Sciences Department of University College at the University of Florida. Each of these opportunities aided me not only in keeping body and soul together but in providing an environment in which the skills of analysis, writing, and research could be further developed.

Special mention should be made of Dr. Victor W. Turner, whose work has proved a great source of learning for this student and whose writings have been heavily drawn upon in the following chapters. Dr. Turner read an earlier draft of this manuscript and offered encouragement and suggestions which served to spur the

[6] William L. Partridge, "The Hippie Ghetto," in *The Not So Solid South*, J. Kenneth Morland, ed. *Proceedings of the Southern Anthropological Society* 4: 74–81, 1971.

preparation of the present work. Likewise, Drs. George and Louise Spindler have given freely of their time and experience in an effort to make this work both readable and relevant.

Finally, thanks is expressed to my informants, whose patience with an inexperienced field worker was remarkable. For it was they who made possible this work, who opened their doors to me, invited me to participate, and explained to me the nature of their community. Many understood fully the nature of my task and the reasons which lay behind my questions, and many actively assisted me in such a way as to make possible the eventual completion of my work. Without such receptivity and cordial acceptance of my role as researcher my efforts would have been made much more difficult and perhaps impossible.

WILLIAM L. PARTRIDGE

Gainesville, Florida
July 1972

Contents

THE HIPPIE GHETTO

1 / The place

THE GHETTO NEIGHBORHOOD, THE TOWN,
AND THE STATE UNIVERSITY

The hippie ghetto is located in a deteriorating low-rent section of what we will call "University City," a college town of about 60,000 people. (This figure applies to the period of study, 1967–1968; today it is close to 90,000.) Though strikingly urban in contrast to its immediate neighbors, University City is similar to many small towns in the South where commerce, economics, politics, and almost all other aspects of daily life are affected by the presence of a single industry—a textile mill, phosphate plant, or tobacco market.

"State University"—which prides itself on being the oldest, largest, and best of the state's universities—remains University City's only major industry. The signs which mark the city boundaries proclaim "Welcome to the University City." Once each year the relationships between the town and the university and the state and the university are expressed symbolically in gala homecoming festivities. Every fall the centrality of State University in the life of the town is recognized on the day the stores and shops close their doors at noon and the populace lines the main street to witness the homecoming parade. And the importance of the university to the state is expressed as Democratic political dignitaries (most of them alumni) wave from open convertibles that inch their way through the town. During the weeks preceding the event the stores, shops, service stations, restaurants, bars, and motels flaunt banners welcoming the returning alumni and exhorting the football gladiators to victory over the visiting rivals. In the week immediately before the homecoming the classrooms of the university are desolate places, as all energies are put to the creation of floats and decorations. Many of the town social clubs participate—contributing floats, brightly polished convertibles, and minor politicians. As it winds its way to the county courthouse, the parade symbolically expresses the tangible reality that State University occupies a central position in the life of the state.

Like the state and the town, the hippie ghetto of University City is dependent on the university. For even though the town's beaches, springs, museums, parks, fine restaurants, and historic monuments are of interest to ghetto residents, the university is the only thing "happening" in University City. It is the source of the hippies' very being—their sustenance and stimulus—for Highland County, of

1

Students assemble in the late afternoon on the University campus to meet friends, chat, and plan activities. Music and political speeches were the focus of rallies during the late 1960s, which usually occurred in this location, directly in front of the library. (Photo by Nancy Sterngold)

The "House of Usher" occupies a central location in the neighborhood called "the ghetto" and is typical of much of the low-rent housing utilized by students in University City. (Photo by Nancy Sterngold)

which University City is the county seat, is largely agricultural. Pulpwood companies long ago cleared off the land and left it to southern white farmers. Residents of the ghetto only rarely venture outside of University City, for the rural populace is hostile and viewed by the students at the university as "red-necks." When residents of the ghetto visit one of the cold springs located in the countryside they travel in a group—in a covey of like-minded visitors who, through a show of numbers, can avoid confrontation with the hostile natives. Stories of atrocities committed against State University students are passed on from seasoned seniors to still-naive freshmen—tales of stints in jail, hair-cutting ceremonies presided over by the sheriff of a neighboring town, and trespassing charges brought to the county courthouse. The students who come to State University are the offspring of an urban middle class. A majority hail from the few urban centers in the state, but many others are from cities in other states and all of them share little with the local populace except residential propinquity.

The civil rights crusade in the South during the 1960s exacerbated the normally tense relations between town and gown. The unspoken truce of former times erupted into violent confrontation as students picketed local stores, theaters, and restaurants. Arrests were made and charges pressed. Scalding water thrown at demonstrators by patrons in a downtown restaurant in 1965, swayed an otherwise complacent minority of students into greater efforts to alter the local caste structure. Organizational rallies for the purpose of picketing recalcitrant businessmen became a common activity on the pine-studded plaza of State University campus. When the protest activity against United States warfare in Vietnam came to University City, the town was nicely polarized already. Town residents gasped as students massed on the university campus for teach-ins, love-ins, and sit-ins; as

A frame dwelling located in the ghetto through which many people passed during the period of study, each adding his own decorative touches. (Photo by Nancy Sterngold)

they disrupted traffic with marches to the county courthouse square in order to present petitions and shout slogans beneath the statue dedicated to the Confederate War Dead.

The hippie ghetto was born into such conditions. It is located between the white neighborhoods and the black quarters of University City—in a fringe area characterized by seedy apartments and dilapidated houses. The area is what the Chicago school of urban ecologists would call "an urban zone of transition," an area where immigrant groups have traditionally invaded the urban center, since this zone is the point of least resistance. Evidence of decaying grandeur mixed with signs of the urban slum mark the neighborhood; one can almost visualize the decline of the carriage house behind the majestic main house into a garage, a respectable apartment, and then a crash pad, with the main house itself being partitioned into apartments in the final stage. Here, in the 1960s, lived most of the "outside agitators," the students who devoted much of their time to organizing picket lines, attracting speakers on civil rights and war, and planning demonstrations. In the 1970s it seems anachronistic to speak of these students as a small group of dedicated activists, for the protester appearance—complete with mass-produced wearing apparel, buttons, and placards—is now identified with student life. But it was not always so. In November 1967 only seven students from State University picketed the Pentagon in Washington; whereas more than five hundred made the journey in 1971. The activist group that lived in the ghetto in the 1960s was very much a minority and very much distrusted by the university community and townspeople alike. Unwashed and unkempt, the activists sallied forth to attack

4

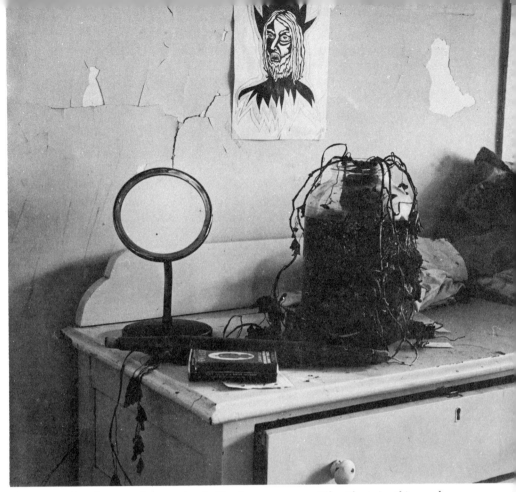

Apartment interiors are frequently shabby in appearance. The plant in this crash pad is neglected since its owner has moved on to another residence. (Photo by Nancy Sterngold)

the sacred cows of segregation and military conquest. In the evening they gathered in one of the bars within walking distance of the ghetto to complain, chart programs, compose poetry for the off-campus newspaper, listen to music, meet lovers, and drink beer.

The large run-down houses of a once prosperous neighborhood provide the residential quarters and in sum create the ghetto. In the center is the "House of Usher," an exceedingly dilapidated barracks-style structure with four apartments on the second level and four on the ground level. The owner of this roach-infested hub of the ghetto lives in a growing metropolis one hundred miles from University City and leaves the management and maintenance of the building to one of its occupants. The management duties and compensation in the form of free living quarters are passed from occupant to occupant. The House of Usher claims the lowest rent of any two-room (bedroom, kitchen–living area) apartment in the city and a location within walking distance of the campus and the downtown area. It sits astride a large sandy lot on Fourteenth Terrace, an oak-lined dirt road

Graffiti on a dining room wall of a ghetto house has accumulated over months and is the product of the efforts of a series of occupants. (Photo by Nancy Sterngold)

between Commerce Avenue and Third Avenue. Along the dirt road are other frame structures with slightly higher rents. At one end of the road is the Hamburger House, an all-night greasy spoon, and an Enco service station. The road immediately fronts the Negro quarters and the rear of a string of shops on Commerce Avenue. A few whites aside from the hippies have stuck it out on Fourteenth Terrace—two families in fact. One block over is Fifteenth Street, also lined with low-rent apartment buildings. Half of the buildings on Fifteenth are occupied by hippie ghetto residents, or "students" as the landlords and townspeople prefer to call them when the rent is at stake. Several of these buildings also have absentee landlords and are managed by a series of occupants. Fifteenth Street is a main artery of the town, linking the northwest white neighborhoods with the southwest white neighborhoods.

The State University campus is three blocks to the west of the hippie ghetto.

Downtown University City is ten blocks to the east. These two areas are linked by Commerce Avenue with the ghetto in between, nestled off the neon lights and blinking signs, of busy Commerce, hidden from view by the traffic of cars and streams of students shopping in the string of shops that leads to the courthouse square. The hippie ghetto is secluded beneath huge oak trees and small clumps of other hard woods which are scattered between the frame buildings. On each side of the House of Usher are expansive "parking lots" dotted with oaks and junked cars. These shaded sand lots are the scene of ghettowide gatherings such as football games, rummage sales, parties, picnics, and political rallies. When a situation that calls for an assemblage of residents arises, one of these lots is the natural meeting site. Everyone knows where the House of Usher is located as well as the Reeberville, the Green Mansion, the Penthouse, and other buildings that are considered more the property of the ghetto social network than of the townspeople who own them. An announcement at the local bar that the party that particular night will be held at the Penthouse (either shouted across the room at closing time or posted on a bulletin board over the jukebox) produces no confusion. Identifying the locality of the party by reference to the current occupant would produce an assemblage of only that person's friends and acquaintances; reference to the building may draw the entire ghetto social network and perhaps some curious visitor.

The dwellings of ghetto residents are modest to run-down in appearance and interiors. Peeling paint, rotten porches and steps, clogged plumbing, paper-thin walls and doors, and flaking, gouged plaster are normal. Furniture is supplied by tenants and landlords in roughly equal proportions. Scrounged chairs and sofas together with homemade shelves and tables usually remain behind when a resident moves. Kitchen equipment and bedding are supplied by the landlord in most cases, and replacement and repairs can be secured if the tenant is patient and very polite. Repairs are temporary and therefore a constant problem. Residents decorate their apartments in what one lighthearted soul described as "late 1940s bargain barn." Furnishings, paintings, sculptures, guitars, refrigerators, and the like are passed down from person to person. When a former resident returns to the ghetto he will demand that his carefully divided possessions be given back to him, but he is usually less than successful. If the atmosphere of life in the ghetto seems communal, since a resident will often point out that he or she got a chair from Jim before he left for Big Sur or a painting from Marsha before she went to Europe, it is only because Jim and Marsha would have difficulty hitchhiking with a chair or painting on their back. The population of the ghetto is highly transient, so that the turnover of possessions is high; objects soon acquire legends and one begins to get the feeling that value accrues with age and the number of hands through which an object has passed. Still, the practice of sharing possessions is less a positive value and more an adaptation to conditions of change.

The high degree of mobility of the population studied is expressed in the practice of sharing possessions. Mobility is a fact of ghetto life that cannot be over-emphasized. At particular times of the year such as the onset of spring or summer practically the whole population is on the move. Some return to University City and others stay in other towns and cities they have discovered during their travels.

Networks of gossip, visiting, letters, and phone calls stretch across the country linking the University City ghetto to other places where hippies have found "good scenes." Such fluctuations in the life of the ghetto are expressed in the social system that has evolved among hippies and much of the ethos of the hippie subculture is directly a product of the transient nature of the life-style. The hippie ghetto is a definite place, a residential area of University City in the South, but it is also much more than a geographical reality. It is a subculture that is defined more by the interaction among its residents than by its spatial location. To this interaction we must now turn our attention.

2/The people

Jules Henry (1965:477) has observed that man's limitless capacity to create misery for himself is what urges him along the evolutionary path. This image is rather grim, but it may not be amiss in the present case. The people described by the label "hippie" are most assuredly miserable. Call it "reform" or "rebellion" or even "revolution," the desire to change the world in which they live is one of their most outstanding features.

Conditions they regard as repugnant, hateful, and sometimes debilitating are daily objects of interest and conversation, although the tone of this interest is one of bitter resignation: For the effects of hateful conditions of existence can be mitigated through selfconscious acts of withdrawal but not wholly abolished. Like Melville's tragic character, Bartleby the Scrivener, who chose to die in jail rather than defend himself, many ghetto residents would simply prefer not to participate. And like Bartleby, they cannot be moved from their self-imposed exile by any amount of urging. For they believe that the hated conditions of twentieth-century America cannot be changed. In particular, many cite with resentment the threats of nuclear annihilation leaders of nations toss across the oceans—an apocalyptic possibility that they feel can no more be affected by responsible participation or dedicated activism than can the arid field be made moist and fertile by the rhythmic chanting and stomping of Hopi snake priests. Given this belief, the task of living is simplified and becomes mere survival. Driven by the ultimate despair of their resignation to helplessness, ghetto residents vacillate between immediate self-gratification ("Don't Die Virgin" read the graffiti scrawled on a university building after President Lyndon B. Johnson began the bombing of North Vietnam) and immediate self-deification ("A Revolutionary Either Wins or Dies," proclaims Ernesto "Che" Guevara from a poster). And if the task of living is merely survival, life is indeed miserable. One benefits nothing by commitment or involvement with other people. It is better to remain apart like the guerrilla fighter, secure within the interstices of society, free to move at will. As one devotee said, "I'll never do anything I don't want to do again"—a remark expressing at once the painful mixture of human dignity and egocentrism that is the newly independent adolescent.

What is a "hippie"? The answer is not very clear if one tries to dissect the strange

9

conglomeration of Christian mysticism, Vedic teachings, revolutionary tracts, Madison Avenue pop-psychology, hedonism, pseudo-American Indian religiosity, and the particularly American virtues of Horatio Alger such as individualism, independence, and frontier courage. Such a piecemeal assemblage from the world's cultures is less a symbolic concatenation of an emergent counterculture and more the clear evidence of an agonizing disorientation. Rather than contribute to the confusion, we will momentarily set aside any attempt to define hippies on the basis of ideology, politics, or symbolic behavior. The reason for this is twofold. First, as any resident of San Francisco will testify, there are many different hippie cults and many different kinds of hippies. With blinding speed these groups and individuals seize an element from the constellation that makes up the cultural universe and devote their total energies to its development and elaboration. And so there are drug groups, nudist groups, vegetarians, communes, Jesus freaks, Krishna devotees, and virtually hundreds of other subdivisions of the larger group called hippies. Second, a definition of hippie is elusive because of those who link their particular ambitions, causes, crusades, and advertising campaigns to the plight of "alienated youth in America today." Conservatives, radicals, liberals, evangelists, and city hall all claim to sympathize with and provide leadership for "alienated youth." For these reasons we cannot be satisfied with a categorical or typological definition of hippie.

We must trace and understand the process by which those who call themselves hippies arrive at a definition. We must understand how these individuals come to identify themselves as hippies. For only as we come to understand the process of social and cultural life, can we see the mutability of categorical and typological definitions. And in order to identify and follow these processes we must begin with the fact that the residents of the hippie ghetto in University City either are students or were students at State University.

The residents of the ghetto were in the process of severing their ties with their families of orientation during the early and middle sixties. One weekend the family either made the long journey to the campus or took its offspring to the airport. In any case the family deposited its charge in a new world. From that moment the charge—henceforth to be called "student"—began the second leg of a journey which moved him from his family of orientation into the "corporate society" (Kimball and McClellan 1966:183). The ties that remained were economic and sympathetic. Like a boat towing a water skier, the family can't carry its charge ashore. It can only skirt near the shore, circling until the skier drops the rope.

The social, political, religious, and economic changes which have occurred since World War II in the United States and in the world have transformed the nature of American society, and with it the socialization and education of the younger members of that society. The central and most momentous transformation has been the industrialization of agrarian America, and the concomitant rapid growth of urban America. The implications of this transformation are broad, but we should be mainly concerned with the impact of this process upon the adolescents who crowded into the institutions of higher learning in the 1960s. Some four million strong they came, and the impact of their numbers is only beginning to be felt throughout the larger society. And as they swarmed in the courtyards, halls, and classrooms, one can imagine that the image of the classical scholar became a little irrelevant. As Kimball and McClellan (1966:138–139) observe, choice of career, choice of mate, choice of companions, and the myriad other choices open to the adolescent in urban America are to be made hastily and spontaneously. The pragmatic image of intelligence operating in decision making—that of the pedestrian encountering a fork in the road and appraising all conditions indicative of the consequences of his choice—used by John Dewey and William James, is anachronistic in modern America. Kimball and McClellan point out that there are in fact a large number of alternative routes and that instead of encountering a fork only once in the course of a stroll, the individual finds that the path is forked every few steps. The result, they point out, is men and women "more conscious of the need to continue in motion than of the direction in which they are going or of the reason for moving at all" (Kimball and McClellan 1966:139).

Perhaps it will not come as a shock to recognize that most educational curricula are designed upon the older model of agrarian America, one in which choice is made leisurely, intelligence is acquired gradually, and Plato is interesting. Today students feel books such as *The Republic* are quaint, intriguing, but irrelevant. What is relevant to students in urban America? This is a question for another book, but it might be correct to say that what is relevant in educational curricula is that which moves the student from his private family into the public world. That is to say, relevant curricula augment and supplement the motion of modern urban America. These curricula decry the "other-directed man" or the "alienated" or "isolated" individual as well as the "mass society" in which Americans are doomed to live out their dreary and dry lives—such is the popular view of the modern world. Educational curricula which teach that the intelligent man contemplates his navel in order to escape the maddening hustle and bustle of the modern world are irrelevant to today's student, although some students find it entertaining to disdain participation in the modern world. The adolescent growing up in urban America seeks to join society and to work to influence its destiny. From the educational institution he demands the tools to accomplish these objectives.

The people who live in the hippie ghetto under study are adolescents of both sexes and are students. The significance of their age and sex will become apparent, but it is important to emphasize from the beginning that the ghetto population is composed of transient students and former students who have consciously cut themselves off from the larger society and are admittedly seeking alternatives to it. They have left their families of orientation with the intent of finding a career or the proper training for a job, of finding a mate, and of finding companions and friends. Apparently, these students have despaired of finding these things within the context of university education and the larger society. Never stable for very long, the ghetto population can be characterized as being in a constant state of flux; the individual might be characterized as being in a constant state of searching or seeking. The ghetto population studied by this observer is now dispersed. The buildings remain and the area is still occupied by hippies. Other areas of the city have since sprouted hippie populations, but the area studied is still referred to as the ghetto. When I returned to visit the ghetto three months after moving away, I found only seven familiar faces in the neighborhood. Those I had known as friends and informants had either found jobs, mates, and companions or had gone to some other town to look.

Unlike the Haight-Ashbury district of San Francisco, made famous by the media coverage of the "hippie movement" in 1967 (Brown 1967), the University City ghetto area is mainly residential and lacks a commercial element. The shops that front the neighborhood are in the hands of "straights" (those who work an eight-to-five job and use only socially acceptable drugs such as alcohol). The majority of these shops do not cater to a "hip crowd." The single exception is the local bar—the only white middle-class bar in town where one might see a racially mixed couple. The bar serves a clientele associated primarily with the ghetto, and its patrons are almost uniformly labeled "freaks" (indicating, usually, shoulder-length hair on males). There is no "strip" in the ghetto to accommodate a street life; hippies in University City congregate mainly in the bar, in residences, on porches, behind doors, on back steps. Panhandling is a rarity, for there are no tourists in the ghetto.

Travelers from other hippie communities tell of the ghetto's reputation in other places. Some visitors heard in New York from some former residents of the ghetto that University City is a "good scene" and a place that is quiet and "not uptight." The local establishment, police, and politicians are reputed by many travelers to be fair, in contrast to the universally despised Oakland, Los Angeles, and New York "pigs." One ghetto resident met some kindred souls living in a brightly painted school bus in Mexico who knew of University City. Another—passing through after a tour of Europe on his motorcycle—spoke of a fellow he met there who had frequented the Tavern, the name of the hip bar until July 1967. Yet while the University City scene is purportedly "cool," it has a major drawback for the hippie population. Jobs are scarce for people who appear strange and eccentric, that is, for people called hippies or freaks. Eccentricity in itself is not uncommon on the university campus. For many it becomes a uniform, much the same as certain brand-name shirts and ties become the uniforms of college fraternity members. But the student uniform of the late 1960s and early 1970s—the hippie-protester appearance—had not yet taken on its faddish proportions at the time of this study. Popular costumes in the ghetto included bell-bottom trousers for both sexes, military uniforms and insignia, ruffled shirtfronts and balloon sleeves, beads of various designs, shoulder-length hair often held in place by a headband, wide belts with heavy brass buckles, felt hats, cowboy boots, motorcycle boots, sandals, both pubic-level and ankle-length hemlines on females, vests, leather pouches, and various forms of costume jewelry. Embroidered butterflies and flowers on jeans, the braless look, peace symbols, and unbleached muslin shirts and blouses were not as common as they are now. To the natives of University City the residents of the ghetto appeared to be atypical, unwashed, and ragged dropouts. Some of them were not. A classification only on the basis of dress or costume would tell us little.

And if classification on the basis of costume tells us little, classification on the basis of social class, religion, and individual background would tell us still less. For it will become apparent that the people who lived in the ghetto were markedly dissimilar. Both Jews and WASPs were represented, with the WASPs forming the bulk of the population. Catholics were present in smaller numbers. Individual backgrounds and social-class origins were highly mixed, with the offspring of waiters and construction workers mingling with the children of university professors and corporation executives. There were few blacks living in the ghetto, and those present usually passed through the ghetto relatively quickly.

QUASI-BANDS AND INDIVIDUALS INTRODUCED

In order to demonstrate this point let us look at one of the groups we will refer to in Chapter 3 as a "quasi-band"[1]—a group of individuals who are more striking in their heterogeneity rather than in their similarity. Jesus—a name adopted somewhere in a past that he was reluctant to discuss—arrived in University City with his wife in a broken-down car that he had nursed through the long trip from California. He had once been a college student but had turned to the hippie life-style and began making sandals for students. He worked for a few months on a contract basis, driving around town in his car and stopping at the apartments or houses of his customers. He would measure their feet, note their choice of style, and return some days later with the finished products. Jesus finally rented a shop and opened a legitimate business; he could be found there at around ten o'clock in the morning and often could be seen working late at night. Business was steady and picked up after a rocky beginning, and eventually Jesus was able to provide employment for Chuck and a few other itinerant leatherworkers. When the orders began to pile up Jesus would turn over some of the work to Chuck on a contract basis. The little business was booming and it looked —at least temporarily from the observer's point of view—as though the leather shop would become an established business in the University City downtown area. (The observer relished the idea of Jesus, bearded and unwashed, wearing his dye-stained T-shirt and torn jeans, speaking at the annual Jaycees' banquet at the local Holiday Inn. Alas, this whimsical possibility never came to pass.)

At the end of the period of research, Jesus's leather shop was doing well. This was a fact that piqued the interest of the researcher. The leatherworking enterprise was intrinsically interesting, but the circumstances surrounding it were more so, for Jesus was a confirmed user of "hard" drugs (heroin, cocaine, and particularly morphine). Chuck, an ex-student from State University, was a part-time leatherworker and a part-time drug dealer who handled most hard drugs in tablet or pill form. Sometime during the day and every evening, Jesus, his wife, Chuck, Martin, Patrick, Carol, and some others who were simply hangers-on would gather and "do up" (inject intravenously with a syringe) from one-to-three "hits" (customary dosage determined by individual tolerance and preference, which varies

[1] The term "quasi-band" refers to a form of human grouping observed in the ghetto. It is drawn from Linton's (1936) and Service's (1962) treatments of band characteristics, including the following: a unit based on residence, with carefully defined boundaries, basically an economic unit, in which membership is reinforced periodically through ritual and ceremonial events.

considerably from one person to another). The observer was present on repeated occasions when this ritual was enacted. Few questions were tolerated when it became apparent that he was not participating, so none were asked. On these occasions the observer was present by a matter of chance; the visit and conversation having to do with something else would simply be interrupted by Chuck's appearance with a bottle of pills, a syringe, and a spoon. The ritual would take place and further conversation was impossible as the participants each experienced, separately and solitarily, the "flash," or what Feldman (1968:136) describes as "the odd combination of a cocoon-comfort and an inexplicable physical ascendency to a 'high.'" The flash past, the all-important "high" achieved, Jesus and his little group would be beyond reach for thirty minutes to an hour depending on the dosage. During this period the participants communicated with each other using gesticulations, nods, and smiles with a minimum of verbal effort (see Foulks and Eisenman 1969:393–394). The observer, unable to communicate because he was not a participant in this ritual, usually left promising a visit at a later time and always feeling that no one else in the room could care less whether he stayed or went or ever returned.

And still the leather shop survived throughout the period of study. The drug-using proprietor and his friends never appeared to proselytize their particular adaptation to the larger society, although their network of friends and fellow users grew slowly until about five males were doing contract work for Jesus out of the shop. Several weeks after the study ended, Chuck was arrested with his girl friend for possession of cocaine and morphine. Jesus left town shortly thereafter and the leatherworking enterprise quickly died. Martin, Patrick, Carol, and the other members of this drug-using group, stayed in University City after Jesus left, attempting to support their habits through the sale of hard drugs. But the market was too small to suit Martin and Patrick, who eventually left town for other, more lucrative urban markets. Apparently University City reached a saturation point of hard drugs in late 1968 such as that reported in other areas (Klein and Phillips 1968). This much is implied, since Martin and Patrick felt the market was too small and not expanding rapidly enough. Carol did not leave town with the others. She "ODed" (overdosed) and died during a visit to another urban center in the southern part of the state.

Most observers would agree that Jesus, his wife, Chuck, Martin, Patrick, and Carol were hippies. They made their living by making sandals and selling drugs. They used LSD, marijuana, and opium in addition to heroin, cocaine, and morphine. They dressed in sandals, bell-bottom jeans, tapered jersey and silky satin shirts of loud colors or complicated designs, and so on. Both sexes wore their hair shoulder-length or longer. Their apartments flickered with neon lights, strobe lights, and day-glow posters; a stereo record player continually droned in the background and a water pipe with multiple hoses and mouthpieces for smoking marijuana occupied a central location on the living room floor. Jesus, his wife, Chuck, Martin, Patrick, and Carol were a quasi-band typical in many respects, atypical in others, of the hippie ghetto. These people should not be considered a typical quasi-band, for the variations in the kinds of social activities, events, and relationships which exist in the ghetto are marked. It will become apparent that it is difficult to categorize the "hippie type" or the "hippie personality." For this reason it is important to stress the contrasts between some of the individuals who make up the social groups living in the area known as the ghetto.

Jesus was from California, where he had been a college student. The circumstances surrounding his decision to learn the trade of sandal making are obscure. He once remarked that he had been very good at arts and crafts in a summer camp where he had been sent as a child. Jesus had a police record in two states— one for drug violations and one for auto theft. His object is coming to the South was to keep a very low profile during the year to come. He had had to sell his motorcycle to finance the journey. His wife rarely spoke, but she came from a suburban community in California and had married Jesus only shortly before they left together for University City. They had no children. Patrick had a wife and a small child, but they were never seen in the leather shop or at the drug rituals. They also came from California and had followed Jesus and his wife to University City. Since the observer met them only once, he found out little about Patrick's family. Martin was the son of an insurance salesman in a major southern city and had fled home in his late teens by joining the navy. He frequently expressed hatred for his family. In the navy he had learned to like morphine. He entered college just after leaving the service but stayed only two terms before dropping out and beginning his drug sales and leatherworking enterprises. Chuck was the son of a middle-class family in Miami Beach. His father sold men's clothing, and he was consequently the style-setter of the group. Chuck had attended State University for four years and received his bachelor's degree in business management during my period of study. He had originally intended to return to his father's store and help run the business, but during my period of study he spoke only of moving to a city where it would be easier to make a good living marketing drugs. During the summer months Chuck worked in hotels as a waiter, a job that provided enough money to return to school and still left significant funds for a capital investment. Carol was one of two members of this group who came from the state in which University City is located. She came to the State University as a freshman and met Chuck in the local hip bar. She studied nothing in particular except Chuck, and her death from an overdose came as a great shock to him. He mourned her loss for several days before leaving University City with Patrick and his family.

Another quasi-band was made up of Richard, Bob, Susan, Diane, Tom, and Judy. This group differed greatly from the one centered on Jesus. Richard was on probation during the period of study. Aged twenty-seven, he was one of the older residents of the ghetto and had been involved in minor crimes for some years. He had begun his college career in 1958 but soon found working on offshore oil rigs more to his liking. After accumulating some money in this fashion he moved to University City, where he enrolled at State University. Richard worked for two years on an off-campus student publication called the *Charlatan*, writing jokes and small articles and drawing a few cartoons. The magazine was a ribald and irreverent rag which delighted the student body at State University, and its sales were quite high. Eventually the editor of the *Charlatan*, who had always taken a critical view of state legislators and university administrators, blasted the university's administration in a particularly defamatory article. He was sued and the publication soon collapsed. Richard talked for a while of assuming the editorship and carrying on single-handedly, but finally gave up and took the first of a series of part-time jobs. His probation resulted from his arrest while "liberating" a refrigerator from an abandoned Negro shack close to the ghetto. Since he was on probation Richard never kept drugs in his apartment, leaving them instead with his girl friend Judy. Judy had come from the southern part of the state to University City as a freshman. Her father owned an automobile dealership in a large city, and her family visited her frequently. Judy's father disapproved of Richard and disapproved of Judy's plans to continue to graduate school upon graduation (still several years off at the time of this study). One got the impression after being around Richard and Judy that their relationship was one of convenience—Richard being a symbol of Judy's independence from her family's plans for her and their periodic reiteration of those plans through weekend visits to University City. Tom and Diane and Bob and Susan were two other couples who associated with Richard and Judy. They often planned parties for each other and gathered together practically every night of the week to smoke marijuana and socialize. Tom sold drugs for a living and was a student at State University. He specialized in marijuana and amphetamines, staying clear of hard drugs and LSD. Diane was likewise a university student. Tom was an "army brat" and had been an avid surfer before coming to University City. He planned to finance the rest of his education through the sale of marijuana and pep pills. Tom believed that "There will always be a black market." He had gotten his first lessons in black market merchandizing by working in a surfboard shop in California where he "fronted [sold] boards that somebody would cop [steal] off the top of a car at the beach." Bob and Susan came from the same hometown and had been living together, like Tom and Diane, since they had been able to leave the dormitories at State University. During the period of study Bob tried to avoid the draft by feigning drug addiction, but he did not succeed. Tom secured a bottle of dexadrine, which Bob used up in the three-day period before his draft physical. Bob attempted to convince the army physicians that he used amphetamine habitually, but a month later he received a letter stating he was physically fit for military service. Susan was distraught and Bob was at first a little hysterical and then became despondent. Tom and Diane and Richard and Judy tried to comfort them, but to little avail. Some weeks later Susan and Bob parted, and she rented an apartment after obtaining a part-time job as a waitress in a downtown restaurant. A few weeks later Susan had lost all contact with the group and had been found by another boy, Lee, who was a successful budding architecture student at State University. Everyone in the group agreed with Bob that Susan's behavior was bad and her character questionable.

Richard, Judy, Tom, Diane, Bob, and Susan spent as much time together as possible. It often seemed to the observer they had no other friends. While Tom, Diane, Judy, Bob, and Susan were all in school, Richard worked part-time. The evenings when they gathered were filled with rather depressing conversations, usually led by Richard, centering on the material and crass nature of American society, the anonymity of urban life, the loneliness and isolation of modern man, and the depravity of a civilization that permitted such atrocities as discrimination, war, and pollution to kill us all. Richard had a wealth of such material and the other members of the group were gradually picking up evidence to prove his point in their studies at the university. Upon occasion Judy or one of the others would be able to offer support to Richard's pessimistic opinions from a course she or he was taking, a book purchased that day, or a campus event. The conversations were gloomy, and when Bob was drafted this became clear evidence of the injustice of modern life. Anyone listening in for a moment would have assumed that they were a most unhappy lot.

Danny was a photography student who lived with Martha. She was a topless dancer at a local bar and had left school some time before the period of study. Danny was a successful art student who dabbled in music and painting. Together with Bill, Mike, and Marty, Danny formed a little combo, or band of stringed instruments—guitar, bass, banjo, and fiddle. On the occasions when they could be coaxed to stage a presentation a good-sized crowd would gather, bottles of wine would be produced, marijuana would be passed around, and the music would continue for several hours. Often, parties such as these were ghettowide functions. Danny's parents lived in a nearby urban center, where his father operated a liquor store. Bill and Marty were students whose parents were suburban dwellers employed by large firms in a city in the northern part of the state. Marty had dropped out of school several times and had worked at various jobs, sold drugs for a short while, and devoted most of his time to his guitar. His father was a university professor at State University. Each of the members of this quasi-band had girl friends at various times during the study, but only Danny lived with his girl friend. Theirs was the only comparatively stable relationship which survived throughout the period of study.

This introduction to the individuals who lived in the ghetto could continue for several more pages and it would become even more evident that the residents were a remarkably heterogeneous group. This book is about their shared behaviors. The foregoing represents a hint of the diversity. Nothing has been said of John, who lived the first years of his life in Greenwich Village and whose mother introduced him to marijuana at about the age of seven. The son of a relatively poor family, John received his master's degree during the period of study. Nor has anything been said of Rick, whose father was wealthy enough to be able to buy University City. Rick carried a stack of credit cards in his father's name and frequently invited the observer and other residents of the ghetto to dinners and wine parties. Rick was working on his Ph.D. degree and finished it several months after the period of study. Neither has mention been made of Fred and Carol, both of whom became dedicated vegetarians and traveled to Pakistan with a Krishna devotee who was passing through University City. Nor have we met Cris, who worked her way to a bachelor's degree as a cocktail waitress. She divorced her husband shortly after enrolling at the university and then gained a rather colorful reputation for her sexual skills before she settled down into a very domestic existence with a graduate student. Neither have we introduced Barbara, a divorcee who worked as a key punch operator at the medical center while earning her degree; nor Jane, who raised two children on her small earnings at the local hip bar after her husband had left her; nor Susan, who left home periodically and took up residence in the ghetto with one of the transient males until she got bored and returned to her husband. And we have not mentioned Marcia, who moved into the ghetto with four males in a four-room apartment after leaving the dormitory at State University. Marcia felt the four males had done her a great favor by taking her in. She did the cooking and cleaned the house for her roommates in exchange for free room and board. Marcia reported that "they're neat guys . . . all smoke [marijuana] and have long hair." She explained that this had become a necessary arrangement when her parents took away her credit cards in retaliation for her leaving the State University dormitory. (She was lucky enough to have spent $480 on clothes before this mishap.) Moreover, her parents would not give her money to rent an apartment. She was convinced that her parents had cut her off in this fashion not only to punish her but also because they were buying another house. Apparently, Marcia's parents were not starving. She once confessed to the observer that she was waiting for someone to come along who she would know immediately was the one with whom she should spend the rest of her life. This she felt proved that she was not "messed up in the head" as some of her friends believed. Until that happy time came she granted her sexual favors to those who cared enough about her to give her room and board. The observer confessed that this seemed like a reasonable approach in the absence of Prince Charming.

These individuals and many more comprised the population called hippies in University City. And they all lived in the area they referred to as the ghetto. Aside from the obvious diversity of their origins, personal habits, values, appearances, and ideals, we can learn very little from further elaboration of the individual inhabitants of the ghetto. Certainly we could compare those who became drug addicts and died with those who were institutionalized. We might give them personality tests, aptitude tests, and directed interviews. And significant data and important similarities might emerge from the apparent diversity in these categories. Likewise, we could concentrate upon sociological information regarding the residents' parentage, social class, school experiences, aspirations, and motivations. These data might also produce significant correlations. And we could provide the same information for those who stayed in school and those who dropped out, those who earned degrees and those who failed to earn degrees, those who used one drug and those who used many different kinds, those who pursued a career in science and those who studied literature or the fine arts, those who had children and those who did not. No doubt there are other important distinctions among these individuals that might be made in relation to significant questions. These kinds of questions are important and deserve answers, but they are not the focus of the present effort.

The central question which will be addressed in the following chapters is one that provides the context for all possibilities suggested above. This central question is the relationship between the people called hippies and the larger American society of which they are both part and product. We will be concerned with the ghetto as part of an ongoing social system and cultural life. Rather than focusing upon the distinctive traits whereby we might classify the various ghetto individuals, groups, relationships, values, and sentiments, we will focus upon the *interaction* among these elements in social life. We will concentrate upon a systematic view of our object of study—one which will discover and demonstrate the interdependencies that exist among the parts of the whole called a social system.

3 / Living and working together

THE RHYTHMIC CYCLE OF GHETTO LIFE

The human life cycle, cultural traditions, and specific environments are significant dimensions of the behavior we call "social organization." The dimension that concerns us now is the social behavior of hippies in relation to the human life cycle. People are not born in the ghetto to live out their full life cycle according to traditional customs, and in this sense we cannot view the ghetto as if it were a fully developed traditional society. The continuous flow of individuals through the hippie ghetto creates special features which lessen stability; yet this flow reveals ghetto life as part of a much larger cultural and social process. This is not to say that people do not reach maturity or have children or die in the ghetto, but that such events must be interpreted in terms of a larger social and cultural setting in which the ghetto is only a minor part.

And the larger social and cultural setting, as has been pointed out in the preceding chapters, is the American educational setting. Basic data of interest to the social scientist involve three questions about his subjects: What are their ages? What are their sexes? What are their social statuses? Hippies are adolescents or young adults, usually from seventeen to twenty-five years of age, and of both sexes. More specifically, residents of the ghetto are males and females who are at the point in the human life cycle when the transition from adolescence to adulthood is to be made. It is at this point in their lives that these individuals have sought out the ghetto as an alternative to "straight society." A more accurate statement might be that the ghetto is sought out as an alternative to adulthood in straight society, for in American society—as in every other society—adulthood is not a biological phenomenon, but a social and cultural one.

Among Irish countrymen social adulthood is achieved quite late in life, sometimes as late as forty years of age. While physiological adulthood occurs twenty years earlier, a man will not be addressed as an adult by his father until he is recognized socially and culturally to be an adult. And that time comes when he owns his own land, directs the farming activity upon it, and finally takes a wife. And among the traditional Kpelle, Mano, Geh, and other tribes of Liberia social adulthood was achieved only after passage through initiation rites conducted periodically by the Poro or Sande, secret societies possessing magical and religious skills upon which the well-being of all members of the tribe depended. Kpelle, Mano, and Geh adolescents were inducted into adulthood around the age of physiological puberty, but any given class of neophytes might range from ten to fourteen years of age or older. The initiation rites were staggered—the men's society, or Poro, inducting the boys in one three-year period and the women's society, or Sande, inducting the girls in the following three-year period. Obviously, these rites were correlated with physiological maturation, but it is significant that the status of adulthood was conferred not by the appearance of physiologicial changes, but by social and cultural recognition of these events.

Adolescents in America are treated in much the same way by the society in which they live. While they are physiologically adults in high school, they are not socially adults until they are incorporated into a set of institutional relationships marked by such things as employment, graduation diplomas, and a family of procreation. Some individuals retain the status of adolescence even longer if they choose to pursue careers that require lengthy training in an institution of higher learning. These persons may be twenty-five or thirty years old before they are given the social and cultural symbols of adulthood in the larger American society.

This brings us to a second consideration, that of social status. As mentioned above, ghetto residents all either are students or were students at a university before coming to the ghetto. The status of student is complex. The world in which students live is one of almost constant flux. The student, in a subjective sense, is perpetually changing. Everything from eating to sex to learning is relegated to a particular block of minutes. The day is usually divided into fifty- to sixty-minute blocks. But the schedule never works, for it must constantly be shifted in response to examinations, papers, assignments, and interests which invariably demand more than twice the minutes allotted.

The status of student is a transitional one, conforming nicely with the transitional nature of late adolescence. Both as a student and a late adolescent the individual is neither here nor there, neither fish nor fowl: he is always becoming and is not yet being. As Friedenberg (1966:37–39) and Turner (1969:109) have observed, insofar as they lack a definite status, individuals occupying such transitional states are often considered dangerous and anarchical. They are claimed by neither side—not by the status they are leaving nor the one for which they are bound. As such they are under the direct control of no single agent, no single group, but are under their own volition. It may be recognized in this context that ghetto residents have made the decision to drop out of school themselves. Most have good academic records and many go on to obtain degrees after years of absence. The point is that the ghetto inhabitants choose to leave school: they are not cast out.

Whether or not adolescents are viewed as dangerous can be discovered by a quick glance at newspaper or magazine articles on the subject of youth and adolescence. Friedenberg (1966:37–39) maintains that adolescents in general are regarded as a social problem simply on the basis of their identity. That is, American culture defines youth as dangerous in itself. This may help to clarify much of the alarm over those who drop out of college. Reader's Digest (January 1968:59) put it this way in one of its characteristic headlines: "Murder, Rape, Disease, Suicide—The dark side of the Hippie moon has become increasingly visible."

The hippies' age and status point to the world of higher education as an important factor in any explanation of hippie behavior, ideals, morality, or values. The route followed from the "straight society" to the "hip society" begins with a person's decision to drop out of the university; much more than this is required of those who would become part of the hippie social network, but this much is necessary in order to win entrance. And the process of dropping out, it should be emphasized, does not always or necessarily entail physical withdrawal from the campus. The dropout frequently remains enrolled and attends classes. "Dropping out" means a reduction of interaction with groups and individuals involving themselves with academics and studies and an increase of interaction with groups and individuals involving themselves with other interests and loyalties. As a student begins the process of dropping out, his commitment to learning (in the formal academic sense) lessens or disappears. This withdrawal is much more than an official cutting of connections with the university symbolized by termination of enrollment. All academic commitments cease to be central demands on an individual's loyalties; and other demands draw his attention and interest and loyalty, although he may still physically occupy a seat in the lecture hall.

We must understand the nature of higher education in America, for it is evident that the hippie ghetto is born of the educational institution in American society. This is not to say it is a product of the educational institution but of the role education plays in the larger American society. That role is defined here as a "rite of passage" (Chapple and Coon, 1942:285; Kimball 1962; Spindler 1973; Turner 1969:69)—a ceremony that eases transition from one status to another; provides for the transmission of skills, tradition, and ritual; and functions to "reject from elevation into the company of the elect those who fail" (Kimball 1962:274). In American universities the students can be viewed as neophytes who must undergo ritual initiation into the mysteries of the society under the authority and direction of a priesthood known as professors. The students are stripped of previous status and considered roughly equal. They are obliged to undergo "rites of purification"—orientation to the college world and batteries of tests designed to probe their pasts, potentials, and predilections—and "rites of scarification"—tests, papers, speeches, oral reports, oral examinations, and projects. After a specified length of time the students are delivered up by the priesthood to the larger society—each one evaluated and assigned a rank in relation to his fellows; and the graduates are incorporated into American society and take on a wholly new status.

Viewing the world of higher education in this manner may create problems for those who feel education plays many roles in American society. This interpretation of education as a rite of passage is not intended to denigrate its other roles. Quite easily seen is the important function of technical and social training. More obvious still is the role of education in providing basic and applied research personnel for the burgeoning industrial sector of the nation's economy, as well as professional personnel in various fields. More latent perhaps is the important function of courtship, mate selection, and marriage for the elect and leaders of the future. And American educational institutions have several other significant functions. But the one which concerns us here should be that which relates the period of adolescence to the structure of the larger social and cultural processes of which it is a part:

the processes of enculturation, social and biological maturation, and social and cultural incorporation of the individual human being. As Kimball observes:

> . . . the ultimate goal and justification for breaking the continuity with earlier activities and associations, and the enforced period of training and abstention from involvement in mature social life, is justified on the grounds of preparing the individual for the religious, political, economic and social demands which . . . life makes (1962:274).

The transitional status and age of the adolescent student is therefore formalized and ritualized by the structure of the educational institutions. The individual is no longer "son of ———" or "daughter of ———," but simply a student or neophyte. Those who choose to leave this transitional position or drop out might be seen as attempting to mitigate the strains and stresses of a transitional status. In the following pages this will be seen to be very much the case.

THE RELATIONSHIP OF THE GHETTO TO THE TOWN AND THE UNIVERSITY

Before turning to a description of the social arrangements which have evolved among hippies we should first understand the nature of the relationship between the ghetto, University City, and State University, for this relationship and its distinctive features provide the context for understanding the social organization of the ghetto. Using the technique of event analysis, we may define relationships among the constituent elements of a system (Arensberg and Kimball 1965:264). We will now examine a particular event in the history of the ghetto to define just such interrelationships, for the changes observed in the ghetto itself are what testify to the nature of its relationship with the larger society. The event took place during the period from June 1968 to August 1969.

Subsistence problems are acute for newly independent adolescents in general, but they are even greater for minority groups and others who are different by virtue of their appearance. In University City there are few jobs for "longhairs" outside the university. As noted earlier, such eccentricities or affectations are not uncommon on the campus. In the town, however, appearance is a factor in securing employment. At the time of this study only the hip bar, a leather shop, a head shop (a store catering to a hippie clientele), and a service station employed males with shoulder-length hair. Most individuals with long hair sought employment on the university campus either in the bookstores, library, laboratories, or plants-and-grounds department. Even these positions are difficult to secure, if only because university employers are reluctant to hire people who may go back to school at any time. Subsistence problems were dramatized by an event beginning in June 1968. Suddenly jobs were available to heads. Two former residents of the ghetto who had previously operated a small television repair service, "Freedom Communications," had found the necessary financial backing to organize Freedom Cable Television, Inc. Through the social networks of the ghetto moved the news that Freedom Cable Television, Inc., was hiring hippies.

The success of the two former ghetto residents in starting a profitable enterprise whereby they could "do their own thing" had been heralded in ghetto circles for months. When the news of the new company came, enthusiasm was general among residents. John and Steve had finally made it from a small television repair outfit to a genuine hip business competing with straights. Moreover several of the ghetto's older residents, who had not held straight jobs for years, were working for the new company. It must be a good thing, it was felt, if the more recalcitrant dropouts found it palatable. These first hippie employees installed a cable television system in a small town in the northern part of the state. As the system neared completion a franchise was secured for another, and then a third small town. The word then came that the company was going to hire "three full crews of heads . . . no straights, no red-necks."

By the end of summer construction of the third system had begun, and the hippie ghetto had become a labor camp—identical in many respects to the lower-class white residential suburbs of University City. Each morning cars and trucks pulled into the ghetto, doors and windows were beat upon and shaken, and a scruffy and bedraggled labor force was prodded from comfortable beds at an hour most had not seen in some time. They did not mind the working conditions except, perhaps, for the early hours which always come with an "eight-to-five thing," because the job was symbolic of much more than simply the beginning wage of $1.65 an hour. First, there was the aura of a vision that had been realized. The "parabolic antenna" could pull in stations up to six hundred miles away and thus was ideal for small isolated rural towns that desired a large choice of stations. Such towns exist in unlimited supply in the South; and, as the owners of the company pointed out, no other companies in the South could offer a comparable service. Georgia, Florida, Alabama, South Carolina—and eventually even southern California—were to be crisscrossed with parabolas. To many this meant Freedom Cable Television, Inc., was "going to take over the world!" The significance of all of this to the bleary-eyed labor force that lived in the ghetto was that "heads were making it." They were, by their actions and by the apparent success of the owners, proving that hippies could be "successful" like anyone else if they chose to be. One can imagine the relish and delight with which one young man climbed on his tractor, a broad red headband holding back his shoulder-length hair, his bell-bottom pants over his work boots, carrying his lunch pail painted with seven or eight different day-glow colors and containing four or five marijuana joints to be smoked during the day.

Second, the various work crews operated by a unique system called the "freedom method." The method consisted in accomplishing all complicated tasks, which might call for speedy decision making and efficient thinking, while one was straight, that is, not stoned on grass. Tasks which were simply routine—like shovel work, measuring out 200 lengths of aluminum wire each 275 feet long, or drilling 6000 holes—could well be accomplished stoned. The managers of the company and the crew foremen were all heads also, and the workers felt their bosses fully realized that marijuana smoking was not like drinking: one could be stoned on grass and still function, although it was generally recognized that normal mental processes were somewhat hampered. Apparently the owners of the company agreed with this idea, for employees and employers alike used the term "freedom method" to express the ability of hippies to make a living on their own terms.

By June of the following summer the ghetto was completely emptied of its male population during the day. Franchises had been picked up for four more small towns in two other states. The word spread over the grapevine. Phone calls were made, positions lined up. People hitchhiked in from the West Coast, Atlanta, New Orleans, New York, and Miami. Heads were coming to University City to get a "hip job." But the influx had just barely begun when it was abruptly halted.

On August 9, 1969 one employee and two former employees were arrested on drug possession and sale charges. The story made the front page of the University City newspaper and the managers of Freedom Cable Television, Inc., found themselves forced to fire the offending party. Suddenly calls came from the city commissioners of the small towns holding franchises with the company, and the company owners were obliged to appear before commission meetings to explain. It soon became apparent that the freedom method would be amended, but just how was not readily apparent. Within a few days, however, the situation became crystal clear as the individual who had financed the company and who owned a controlling interest in the company stock called a meeting of all employees. He explained that the dress and grooming habits of employees had never been an issue, but now everyone was going to have to look "joe-average." The other stockholders, the founders of the company from the ghetto, remained silent. During the question-and-answer period that followed, the employees bluntly accused the controlling stockholder of placing money before principles. He agreed and pointed out that "Even my lawyer has sideburns down to here . . . this is not New York. . . . We are dealing with bigoted small-town farmers." Employees were instructed to "clean up to a point that you can tolerate" and report back within a week for inspection.

That same night a group of employees tried to organize a strike in the parking lot outside the House of Usher, but most of the ghetto males were not going back to work for the company anyway. Most of the residents merely grumbled "We took this job because . . . and now it's just like pushing hamburgers at McDonald's." One hippie who had quit a job in New York where he had been "hassled about my hair" glumly commented, "Even Freedom Cable TV sells out when the shit starts flying." Within a week all the hippies had quit the company, and the ghetto was once again alive with activity throughout the day and into the night and early morning hours. The hippies who had come from other cities because "the ghetto is a good scene" soon split to find another scene. There was little point in staying, apparently, even if the ghetto had once been a good scene. The residents began looking for other jobs or seeking loans so they might return to school that fall, but 60 to 70 percent of those who had held positions as foremen, shop supervisors, and crew leaders left town to try other scenes. A few weeks after the drug arrests only two ghetto residents remained with the company, and they looked pretty joe-average.

This event and, most importantly, its consequences point out the nature of the hippie ghetto as it is related to State University and University City. Those who live in the ghetto are usually connected with the university; those who cannot or choose not to establish such a connection usually move on. The relationship, then, is explicit: one is either related in some way to the academic world or one is absent from the hippie ghetto. There are notable exceptions who—like the two residents who founded the freedom method—attempt to set up their own businesses in order to secure occupations in the city. And these persons are not rare. During the period of study, that is, June 1967 through September 1968, three coffee houses, two boutiques, a head shop, and numerous rock bands were established by enterprising young hippies from the ghetto only to fail in a matter of months. Only a leather shop and a head shop have managed to persevere, but they have done so only by serving a pseudohippie, or "plastic hippie," crowd from the university campus riding the current fashion wave of "mod" and hip apparel and accoutrements. The Freedom Cable Television incident confirms the fact that the ghetto population is small—too small to support any hippie population independent of the academic world. The lack of jobs for hippies who cannot tolerate a university atmosphere keeps the ghetto population too small to support any business directed to a hippie clientele.

The relationship between the hippie ghetto and the university finds expression in a number of other ways, notably rhythmic changes which have as their source the academic calendar. The rhythm set up by fluctuations in the university's calendar is felt in the ghetto because the majority of residents either work or are enrolled at the university. Simply in terms of a head count the population can be observed to fluctuate from academic quarter to academic quarter.

University-oriented residents, in essence, lead two distinct lifestyles: one during the fall, winter, and spring; the second during the summer months. Life in the hippie ghetto during the fall-winter-spring period begins at dusk. Until that time of day most residents are either at work or in classes. Even those who are not connected in some way to the university conform to this pattern for two reasons: first, they themselves must work in some capacity (an exception is those who sell drugs and, therefore, wait for the return of their customers at dusk); second, their neighbors in the ghetto are mostly academically oriented. Around four thirty in the afternoon people begin filtering into the ghetto. On warm days they will congregate outside; but during the colder months groups gather in various apartments around dusk. The evening is passed conversing, listening to records, and smoking marijuana unless plans to attend an event on campus, see a movie, or the like develop. The latter events are generally generated spontaneously as the group gathers. An expedition is usually mounted, for rarely do residents travel to distant places alone.

Depending upon the activities of a particular evening, from dusk till early morning music fills the ghetto. Out of every building drifts (or blares) the popular music well associated with hippies: folk, blues, jazz, and, of course, rock. Besides drugs of various kinds, the most ubiquitous item associated with ghetto apartments is the stereo phonograph and a well-worn stack of long-playing records. Throughout the night people wander into the ghetto area visiting friends. Most such visits are impromptu and unannounced. This traffic becomes rather heavy at times; but it is not haphazard, for visitors usually have specific destinations. Doors are locked and visitors are not usually welcome if they are unkown. It is not the custom to invite guests to another's apartment; in this way it is felt, residents enjoy a certain amount of peace with regard to the threat of being "busted." The exception to this, of course, is the group that deals in drugs for a living. For these people, all manner of customs regulate the flow of traffic to and from their doors. Most dealers prefer to work through contacts or middlemen; almost none like customers to appear unannounced at their doors. Some will not keep drugs in their apartments and store them outside somewhere; and some prefer to deal at a customer's or a middleman's apartment. A few dealers will sell drugs at any time and in any place—however great the danger—for the tremendous profits that can be garnered through a large-volume business often tend to intoxicate the greedy. As a point of fact, the observer was acquainted with one street dealer (one who sells drugs in small quantities) who turned over $1000 in marijuana and amphetamines in a single week! But selling large quantities of drugs out of a ghetto apartment is quite foolish and also tends to endanger other residents of ghetto apartments. Residents openly expressed resentment at such uncool behavior, although law enforcement agencies had not been known to arrest ghetto residents who simply possesssed small quantities of drugs at the time of this study. (This pattern changed drastically in April 1969.) In general, only those who have dealt in large quantities have been arrested, but the ghetto as a whole tends to become "uptight" when rumors of a bust are circulating. On one such occasion several people hung out signs announcing the bust and one lighthearted soul reportedly left milk and cookies near the door.

With the coming of summer the ghetto changes dramatically. Students cease to be students and begin looking for jobs. Those employed by the university often find themselves unemployed as the budgets of most departments are drastically cut. The population of the ghetto drops significantly as people leave town to travel and seek summer jobs; travelers arrive in town from other areas searching for the same thing that residents have despaired of finding. Entrepreneurial efforts are frequently begun throughout the summer, but most do not take root and the innovators move on. For a period of a month to six weeks the population turnover continues, and it may be safe to assume that other cities witness the same turnover, since the flow of traffic is both into and out of the University City area. All the while that this movement is going on, there occur parties, feasts, and excursions. During this brief period of flux everyone can do his thing twenty-four hours a day. The grapevine tells daily of communes being started, construction projects hiring hippies, and good scenes developing in Denver or Atlanta or elsewhere. Daily life no longer begins at dusk, but late in the morning. Either parties or job-hunting efforts or both are planned throughout the day, and by evening something has generally materialized in the way of a mass celebration often involving forty or fifty people. With the arrival and departure of residents these celebrations may be billed as farewell or welcoming parties for so-and-so, but they occur so frequently and are so large that it is difficult to accept this explanation for them.

The feeling of change is in the air, and it is contagious. Males and females who have been living together, doing a thing, or who have even been married tend to separate and initiate new relationships. Efforts at communal living occur most frequently in the summertime and often such experiments are correlated with the separation of mates. In the summer of 1967 a communal experiment was initiated involving two males and one female, all students or former students. According to stories told by one group, the summer of 1966 was when some ten to twelve persons left University City to begin a commune on Hog Island, a rather desolate piece of sandy island in the middle of a river. Likewise, in the summer of 1968 a commune was planned but never materialized among several couples seeking a change. And in the summer of 1969, three couples split apart and the female members of each took up residence together on a lake some twenty-five miles from the city. Two of the males traveled while the third continued to work in the area and initiated new relations with another female.

The fluctuations in male-female relations and the efforts to establish communes and businesses are probably directly related to the instability of the ghetto population. In view of the changes observed when Freedom Cable Television, Inc., altered the normal relationship between the university and the hippie ghetto, it can probably be concluded that the change in the university calendar in part brings on this summer period of instability and the concomitant innovative life-styles. In general, the summer marks a time of change for most employees of American universities. Both faculty and students on assistantships and scholarships find themselves scrambling for alternate means of support. For those marginally committed to the university such changes are probably all the more unsettling and disruptive, for they do not enjoy even the relative security of knowing that with the coming of fall they will return to University City and resume their former life-styles. And as old ways of living change, the horizon takes on the glow of opportunity in the eyes of both the courageous and the foolhardy. Those with their ears attuned to the grapevine begin to hear it hum.

SOCIAL ORGANIZATION

Building upon the description in the previous section of the rhythmic cycle of ghetto life dictated by the complex relations between the university, the ghetto residents, and the town of University City we can now turn to a discussion of the social organization of the ghetto. The reader might well ask at this point, "What organized social life can exist among people intent upon doing their own thing? And at first glance, observers in the 1960s often concluded that hippie life proceeded in rather unorganized fashion, as the phrase "free love" indicates. But we have already seen that ghetto life is structured by the particular age, sex and social status of the residents. We can also expect certain universal cultural and biological processes to be at work structuring social behavior along certain lines. The transition from adolescence to adulthood has already been emphasized as one of these processes. Obviously, courtship and mating processes as well as the struggle for subsistence are additional considerations indicated by our three questions of age, sex, and status. Also, through examination of a significant event in the lives of ghetto residents—Freedom Cable Television, Inc.—we were able to see that the relationships between the university, the ghetto, and the town are structured by the very definite cycle of the university calendar—the ebb and flow of human beings involved in the task of living being dramatically affected by fluctuations in this calendar. When this relationship was disturbed by the hiring policy of Freedom Cable Television, Inc., the lives of ghetto residents became quite different. In short, the lives of the hippies in University City are quite organized by processes and relationships which obtain between ghetto residents and between the hippie ghetto and other sectors of the population of University City. Moving one step further we must ask: What is the social organization of the ghetto itself—granting that this organization is dictated in part by the place of the ghetto in a larger social and cultural context? Turning the well-worn phrase "dropping out" around, we must ask: What does the hippie drop into? The route followed from the straight world of higher education to the hippie ghetto begins with the individual decision to drop out. But our concern here is not so much with the nature of this decision or the reasons for it as with the nature of its consequences—being inducted into ghetto society.

Any discussion of social organization begins with a classification of social units, the sum of which are called the society. Normally, anthropologists have found the family to be the smallest unit of social organization, though not always the most important unit in terms of the organization and perpetuation of social life. An example is Pygmy social organization where the social form called a "band"—a seemingly loose agglomeration of families held together by common residence, economic cooperation, and almost daily enactment of rituals—clearly plays as important and vital a role as does the family (Turnbull 1961). And in the present instance the smallest unit is not the family. Not all ghetto residents have mates, and only a minority have offspring. And almost all residents have severed or are attempting to sever ties with their families of orientation. The characteristic units of social organization in the ghetto are the pair relationship and the quasi-band. A "pair relationship" is rather simple to explain: two individuals who maintain customary patterns of interaction for specific events and under specific conditions. The "quasi-band" however is not so easy. Anthropologists have generally understood the "band" to be a local group held together through common residence rather than kinship, having a simple internal structure, possessing a rather simple technology, in which group boundaries and standards of correct behavior are sanctioned by the forces of ridicule and gossip, which are likely to have headmen for certain functions, which periodically assemble with other bands to form tribes, and in which the identity of band members is periodically reinforced and expressed through ritual and ceremonial events (Linton 1936:210–230). Such groups can often become quite large, as they did among the Andaman Islanders in Australia; the Yahgan of Tierra del Fuego; and among the Sioux, Cree, Cheyenne, Crow, and Arapaho on the North American Great Plains (Service 1962). The term "quasi-band" has been used here to denote certain similarities between hippie social organization and the band form of social organization, with which anthropologists are quite familiar. The hippie group is called a quasi-band because in the ghetto this form of organization does not include some of the characteristics normally associated with the band level; that is, that the band is found among primitives and is linked to a simple technology of hunting and gathering. The writer is convinced, however, that this term drawn from anthropological terminology is the best for conveying the realities of the hippie ghetto social form: one in which membership is determined on the basis of residence and not kinship, in which group boundaries are carefully maintained and correct behavior enforced, which is an economic unit, and in which membership is periodically reinforced through ritual and ceremonial reintegration. We will return to a more thorough discussion of this hippie social form in a moment. First, we should understand how pair relationships come into being and then we can turn to the ways in which these units are knit into the larger social units called quasi-bands. In order to demonstrate the pair relationships, it is useful to trace the history of a hypothetical initiate as he enters the ghetto, passes through a period of socialization, and finally leaves the ghetto. For purposes of discussion, then, we will speak of stages of development. But in reality the pattern of hippie ghetto life does not admit of such a neat model, for neophytes seek out the ghetto almost constantly and their presence always introduces an element of disorganization into the tightly knit ghetto society. There are two important types of pair relationships found in the ghetto: "elder-neophyte" and "male-female." We will consider the elder-neophyte relationship first.

ELDERS AND NEOPHYTES

Hypothetically, a person who chooses to join the ghetto population can do so in one of two ways. First, he might rent an apartment in the neighborhood, but this is actually very difficult given the fact that the managers of the apartment buildings are themselves members of ghetto society. They prefer to pass on an apartment to another ghetto person or another head, to a friend or the friend of a friend. This arrangement is fine with the absentee owners, for the rooms are always full. One never sees advertisements in the newspapers for apartments in the ghetto: they are filled by ghetto society. So the vehicle for entrance into the ghetto is through the social networks of ghetto society. Friendships made at the local hip bar or in academic departments or radical political groups function in this way. The members of the group will keep their ears open for someone moving and inform the neophyte of vacancies, for the population is quite mobile and apartments become available at odd times. There are many more people in the ghetto social network than there are residences in the ghetto neighborhood. Apartments, then, are at a certain premium and, more significantly, are unavailable to those outside the quasi-bands of ghetto society.

Upon moving into the ghetto residential area the neophyte begins a period of socialization, learning the customs and beliefs of the social group which has admitted him. It is here that the associational group obtains an intimate view of the neophyte's life and that sanctions and controls can be enforced through the well-known devices of gossip and ridicule. The credo "do your own thing" calls for a conscious and determined effort to experiment; and during the time of this study residents of the ghetto generally felt themselves involved in a mission to seek alternatives to the larger American society—a society they viewed as hypocritical, warlike, and inherently evil. Experimentation calls for the conscious breaking down of social inhibitions and restraints, for the hippies felt that only when these controls upon social behavior are lifted can an individual discover what his thing may be. Socialization, then, is said to take place in an atmosphere of freedom, freedom to experiment in the absence of responsibility for one's actions. Freedom from responsibility is seen as a critical aid to the expression of things that might have been suppressed or subliminated due to the influence of straight society. *Experiencing, experimenting, freeing oneself, learning*: These are the often-repeated words used by ghetto residents to describe their first weeks in the ghetto. One neophyte's comment is typical of most with whom I talked.

> I've been in school since I was five years old. I'd never considered anything but the next grade, ever onward and upward. This is beautiful because I'm digging what I want, not just what's next in line.

From the standpoint of the neophyte, then, the first few weeks spent in the ghetto are a period of freedom and experimentation, discovering likes and dislikes, painting canvases, protesting the war, making love, using drugs, and perhaps leaving school and books behind for a while. Of course, many students at State University discover likes and dislikes, paint canvases, protest the war, make love, use drugs, and forget about books once in a while. What makes the ghetto different? Quite simply, only one thing: the importance of "elders." The neophyte soon learns that the quasi-band through which he gained entrance into the ghetto is composed of neophytes like himself and older ghetto residents, or elders—people to whom problems encountered during this period can be taken, people who have probably experienced and learned to understand many of the same problems. The role of elder is a complex one and deserves some attention. An elder is not that much older chronologically, but acts as a guide and model during the period of experimentation. One learns from him what is "groovy" and what is a "drag." The days are filled with activities and socializing with one's neighbors and friends; the nights are passed in "rap sessions," or group conversations accompanied by drug use. And the elder plays an important role in such conversations, for he speaks from experience and from the past and his judgment carries weight. Long "rap sessions" (see Chapter 4)—centered on the draft, drugs, the larger society, communes, self-knowledge, and myriad other topics—call for information and pronouncements from elders and occupy many hours every evening and into the morning, with the drug ritual a ubiquitous vehicle of communion and of communication.

In the apartment of one elder with whom the observer became acquainted during the first months of study, rap sessions occurred every evening of the week. A seemingly large group of people whom the elder had first "turned on to themselves" passed through as neophytes. He would pass around the sacramental joints, or marijuana cigarettes, and play the new rock groups on the stereo. Acting as advocate, concerned counselor, and salesman, the elder often extolled the virtues of marijuana in "learning about yourself" and "seeing the world as it is." Questions about the drug were answered with confidence, for he had used marijuana for many years. And as other topics came up he led the group in a ceremonial which consisted of introducing examples of hypocrisies and contradictions from the straight world. A popular example in this group—all of whom had been involved in antiwar activity—was "Parents train kids to be responsible, and then when they are responsible—like in protesting the war—parents call it anti-American." Such ironies are entertaining and neophytes are properly entertained; but the message is obviously deeper and might be interpreted as follows: responsibility is good, but it is not to be dictated by parents, politicians, professors, and policemen.

Our concern, however, is not so much with the content of the message as with the mechanics of the neophyte-elder relationship, for this relationship mediates any communication that occurs. A bond is slowly built up between the neophyte and the elders through the process of searching out and discovering the flaws and contradictions of straight society; and the neophyte soon learns that there are many—if he has not discovered that already. In this process the traditions of the ghetto society are given expression in stories told about older ghetto residents who may have moved on or may still be around. Told for purposes of illustrating points or supporting an argument, these anecdotes also serve to illustrate values for the neophyte and to link him into a network of individuals much larger than he may realize at the time. As the group's "ancestors" are revealed to the neophyte, a bond which links him to them is established. By it he will, at some later time, understand his position in the group as he traces his various relationships in a manner not unlike kinship reckoning. "Who turned Steve on?" "Joan first turned on in 1958." The string of persons linking the past to the present explains how the group developed and who is a member of the group. And origins are important, for in addition to explaining who is related to whom they explain who is closer to the almost legendary beginning of the ghetto "when there were only five heads in the whole town." Moreover, the bond established at this stage links the neophyte into a network of like-minded persons who can aid and assist him in the future.

Many of the problems encountered by the neophyte center on sex and subsistence. Given the irresponsible free life-style of the neophyte, it is almost imperative that his physical needs be provided by someone other than himself. The initiate generally does not work, enters and leaves school according to the "shape of his head," and is essentially unproductive. The vast majority of neophytes are still dependent upon their parents for support, so subsistence may not be a problem though the neophyte recognizes that it will be soon. Like problems of subsistence, sexual needs are not a novel invention of the ghetto society, but the context in which these needs are to be solved is new. Just as a change in the relationship of a neophyte to his studies carries the threat that parental support may be withdrawn and he will be on his own financially, moving out of sex-segregated housing at State University carries the threat that decisions about sexual relations must now be made on one's own. Each of these problems (or opportunities, if you will) may appear threatening to the neophyte if he has never confronted them before; and for those who have been incubated in the public educational system for thirteen years or more the decisions to be made are important. It is logical, then, that the elder —who has made such decisions before and who has learned from the many others who have preceded him—becomes an important source of advice and counsel. For the world of the neophyte is a kaleidoscope of opportunities, decisions, and consequences. The conscious decision to seek alternatives introduces a host of stimuli previously sublimated or consciously ignored. One way of organizing this collage is through the lens of the elder's ideals, experiences, and stories, for here it takes on meaning or is given an interpretation which defines and focuses. New to the experience of being stoned frequently on drugs, new to a world where one is free from responsibility, new to the opportunities of freedom of choice, the neophyte may be confused and even frightened. It is the elders who have experience in these matters, who carry on the community's traditions and ideals, and who have the highest status. It is they who give form, meaning, significance, and security to the kaleidoscopic world of the neophyte.

Obviously, induction is a complex procedure. But it is not unorganized nor is it undertaken alone. Those labeled elders have been fully incorporated into the social networks of the ghetto. They have, we are told, left the straight world, dropped out, become self-sufficient and independent. They have come to rely upon their own abilities and upon reciprocal relationships with their fellows to survive in a world that is often seen as hostile. Thus, dropping out is not an act of cutting oneself adrift and merely wandering or becoming a hermit. Rather to drop out is to become a fully participating member of a community of persons who are willing and able to offer help. The problems of subsistence and sex have been mentioned briefly above and deserve further discussion, for the ways in which the ghetto resident finds solutions to these problems provides an interesting illustration of the central importance of the elder-neophyte pair relationship.

QUASI-BANDS

Previously, the neophyte drew support to a greater or lesser extent from his parents. Most ghetto residents are from middle-class homes, and the great majority are being put through school by their parents. Now simply by virtue of continued exposure to the self-reliance and independence of the elders, the neophyte desires to become more autonomous, more fully adult. If this is not the case, a person is frequently forced into this posture by parental rejection. In any event the various quasi-bands which exist in the ghetto offer the neophyte assistance, for the quasi-band usually consists of a number of persons who subsist in the same fashion. For example, one associational group is made up of people who are employed at the bar across from the ghetto neighborhood. When a neophyte became attached to one of the elders in this group, one of the shifts was simply cut in half, and two persons were then employed. Likewise, waitress duties at the bar were shared among a group of three or four females who alternated on different nights so that several people might have at least some income.

There is, then, a high correlation between source of subsistence and the makeup of a quasi-band. Elders are quite important in the life of the group, for it is they who have long-standing friendships with employers, who can act as contacts, and perhaps can even guarantee placement in a position. Nowhere is this more obvious than in drug procurement and sales. Drug dealing—that is, selling drugs in small quantities on the street—is a means of subsistence for several quasi-bands. Most people in the ghetto sell drugs at one time or another; when a person obtains some particularly desirable marijuana or LSD he is generally expected to "turn on" his friends. But not everyone wishes to run the risk of selling to strangers or trying to market drugs on the campus of State University. Those who wish to take such risks—and considering the great profits to be gained they are not rare—form quite tight quasi-bands. Contacts for relatively inexpensive quantities of particular drugs are controlled by elders who can disclose them to the neophyte who wishes to deal as a means of subsistence. Reciprocity relationships and the result, mutual obligation, are quite obviously of some importance here, for it takes a considerable amount of capital and some experience to make a profit in this kind of venture. Neophytes are assisted in securing a safe market, learning appropriate precautions, obtaining the drug itself, preparing and packaging the drug, and cutting the quantity of drug with something to increase profits. The elder-neophyte relationship is obviously of crucial importance to these quasi-bands. Since all residents of the ghetto use drugs, the elder-neophyte relationship in all associational groups works in much the same way. Thus, in the group associated with the bar certain elders obtain for their group members drugs of choice. And it is only after a considerable period of time that contacts for these goods are disclosed to new members of the group. This is not to say that the drug traffic in 1967 and 1968 was tightly controlled by cliques of elders in the ghetto. It definitely was *not* tightly controlled. Marijuana, amphetamines, barbiturates, and hallucinogens could all be purchased readily from the quasi-bands that dealt in these drugs but they were sold at straight prices and were generally cut with foreign matter to increase their weight for street sales. The elders of all quasi-bands are of crucial importance in obtaining inexpensive and high-quality drugs. Buying drugs in the absence of such a relationship is expensive, and can be quite dangerous with some of the hard drugs. One is reminded here of Carol, mentioned in Chapter 2, who died of an overdose when she left University City and bought drugs in a strange town from people she did not know in a strength and quantity with which she was unfamiliar.

Another kind of quasi-band secures jobs at State University. The nature of these jobs is such that a certain level of skill, ability, or education is usually required. Often they are related to training which the individual might have received while he was a student. But, more significantly, contacts and familiarity with the university community are necessary, for positions become available at odd times as funds fluctuate and change from year to year. Elders can offer inside information, contacts, and often influence to obtain positions at the campus bookstore, the museum, laboratories, the medical center, as well as the plants-and-grounds division and the library. At the very least they are able to offer neophytes advice and descriptions of possible jobs and potential employers.

Still other quasi-bands secure a means of subsistence in the context of the business community of University City. Females are usually successful finding jobs as waitresses or sales clerks; males often find it difficult to obtain work except at one service station which hired freaks. The hip bar provides employment for about three males, and the head shop employs only about two males. The leather shop mentioned in Chapter 2 provided an income for several additional males. Opportunities for straight jobs are very few for the ghetto male population, and hip jobs are even more scarce. And at this point it is significant to note that associational groups are often male-centered, with females appended on as sexual liaisons shift. Female-centered groups exist but are short-lived, since their members often develop relationships with males in different male-centered groups. Males tend to cluster into groups more readily, probably because males handle the drug traffic and also because males find subsistence more difficult to secure. Females enjoy a little more success in securing a means of subsistence in University City, and hence do not feel the need for tight associational networks and firm reciprocal obligations; nor do they feel it necessary to keep in close contact with the grapevine in order to stay advised of new opportunities for subsistence-related activities.

MALES AND FEMALES

Relations between the sexes are less influenced by the elder-neophyte relationship than are problems of subsistence. Hippies have been painted as promiscuous by the media (for example, see Brown 1967), and so they are by the standards of the larger society. But our effort here should be to try and understand how this fact is related to other aspects of life in the hippie ghetto. Adolescents are generally concerned with courtship and mating in American society, but sexual activity is usually circumscribed and governed by the custom of dating. The general pattern for American society consists in increasing the frequency of interaction between male and female gradually, with a concomitant decrease in the frequency of interaction with others, until the pair is engaged or otherwise considered a couple. Students at State University develop such relationships in the context of parties, movies, restaurants, beaches, plays, and concerts. Yet in a formal sense the sexes remain segregated in dormitory housing. And while a great deal of foreplay and petting may take place in cars, gardens, and patios, a relationship which includes coitus is difficult in the intimate confines of a dormitory room or fraternity house room. Certainly this is not to say that sexual relations do not occur; it is to say that the sex act is usually possible only in a situation where roommates and friends cannot make bothersome claims upon the same quarters. Hence, complete sexual relationships are difficult and perhaps tedious, since they must be nurtured in an environment designed to inhibit them. And nurtured they are, for it is virtually impossible to inhibit sexually active adolescents.

The ghetto presents to the student at State University an opportunity to consummate a relationship with a person of the opposite sex—a relationship that may include traveling, sleeping, eating, and living together. For those who feel the limitations imposed by the moral standards of the larger society are unreasonable, this kind of sexual relationship becomes almost obligatory. Our hypothetical neophyte will discover after his initial indoctrination and socialization experiences that many if not most residents of the ghetto try to work out such arrangements. Of course, dating occurs constantly, but courtship and mating in the ghetto begin when individuals reside in the same apartment or house, for only when couples live together are they actually considered mates. Even though they may spend almost all their time together while dating, they are merely "doing a thing" informally until they live in the same quarters. In fact, rather stable sexual relationships may obtain for some length of time between a male and female, and they will continue to see other members of the opposite sex and continue to date. For it is not until they actually live together that any kind of formal commitment is made. This is in marked contrast to the sexual behavior of adolescents in the larger society, where dating steadily is considered a commitment.

The ghetto pattern dictates that sexual relationships often shift before a mate is found. And a person normally changes mates several times. One must keep in mind that the neophyte is experimenting with alternatives searching for and finding what he perceives to be an opportunity for a different way of living. Seldom will a mate be found on the first try. Experimentation, then, is considered normative behavior for someone who proclaims himself to be a dropout, becomes part of the ghetto social network, and moves into a ghetto apartment. This pattern is made more clear when it is recognized that females as well as males seek alternatives to straight society. Just as the male seeks to be liberated from the seeming rootlessness of training and preparation for the next step on the ladder of a career, the female seeks to liberate herself from the seeming ignominy of domesticity. Recognizing that career opportunities for females are much greater than in their parents' generation, females must evolve among themselves and for themselves roles, ideas of proper behavior, standards of morality, and so on which have not been provided for them by early childhood socialization, traditional adolescent role models, and cultural ideals and goals. This is especially true for the students who enter the world of higher education directly from high school. Branching out in this manner and experimenting with different kinds of behaviors, ideas, and beliefs means that male-female relationships are often unstable and result in frequent changes of partners. And it should be reemphasized that both males and females are searching for alternative ways of living. For the male, relations with a female will be impossible if he consciously or unconsciously demands dedication or commitment to the traditional domestic role model of the female. For the female, relationships with a male will be impossible if she demands commitment to the traditional steady provider role model of the male. The period of experimentation provides courting males and females with the opportunity to explore the potential of their relationship, the nature of each other's expectations, and the nature of their own expectations regarding a mate. Some residents decide they prefer marriage and a relationship along traditional lines; that is, the alternatives they find are unacceptable. Others conclude they simply must keep looking for the right person; that is, their past relationships have failed, but alternative ways of living still are possible. Still others decide that relationships with the opposite sex are too painful, too time consuming, or too expensive and prefer to live alone; that is, both marriage and playing the field are unacceptable to them. But we are not concerned so much with the actual conclusions reached by ghetto residents as with the process of living and working together that influences these conclusions, whatever they may be. And that process, as emphasized already, is experimentation with and exploration of another person's potential as a possible friend, lover, or spouse. This is what has been called promiscuity, but one might also call it opportunity or a conscious exploration of mutuality.

Experimentation with alternatives to traditional and conventional modes of behavior and value systems means that arrangements between the sexes that develop in such an atmosphere will be fragile. While this may perplex some observers in the larger society, residents of the ghetto consider experimentation of crucial importance. But in any situation involving innovation and change, not all experiments succeed. Not all ghetto residents who seek a mate can easily throw off the traditional sex roles which characterized their earlier experiences. These roles are among the hardest elements of the behavior one learns young in life to alter. Often females who desire an alternative to domesticity, and still desire the intimacy of a relationship with a mate will discover that a particular male demands deference, commitment to household duties, childbearing, and so on, from them. The reverse is often true of males who seek alternatives to the traditional male role of provider. For example, the male who attaches himself to a female who likes playing the role of provider has attained a viable relationship if the female truly enjoys this kind of role reversal. But how can either partner be sure that the relationship will work? Perhaps the female thinks that the male will eventually lose his fascination for oil paints and canvas and get a job. Until that time she may be content to carry the burden of supporting a household—all the while communicating in myriad ways her basic dissatisfaction with their arrangement. Or suppose two persons enter into an arrangement on the premise that the male wants his mate to work and the female desires help in such household duties as washing, cleaning, shopping, and the like. The male may merely have agreed to such an arrangement in order to win his mate but actually prefer a mate that does not work outside the home and is an efficient housekeeper. Each of the partners in this relationship will communicate their dissatisfaction to each other. In short, the flexibility and adaptability of a partner cannot always be discovered simply by dating or doing a thing with him or her. Often a good deal of time is needed to learn about the real wants and needs of the other person and of oneself. The act of mating, then, is not in itself considered binding on either partner. Ghetto residents often feel that the best adjustment to a particular situation is withdrawal or the severance of ties.

But aside from the importance of experimentation as a spoken and conscious ideal, other important factors contribute to the constantly shifting relationships between males and females. First, not all residents are dedicated to experimentation and the development of alternatives to the larger society. Some, for example, are concerned mainly with obtaining drugs. Given the free atmosphere surrounding sexual relationships some individuals offer their sexual services for certain drugs. The same applies to other highly valued items such as trips to rock festivals and answers to exam questions. Second, the transient nature of the ghetto population (noted in Chapter 2), which is rooted in the rhythm of the university calendar and in the stage of life cycle called adolescence, contributes to an atmosphere in which shifting alliances and relationships are perhaps the best way to discover a suitable mate. The person who makes the wrong choice and discovers it will soon be presented with another opportunity to choose. Of course, a person who makes such choices fairly frequently and never seems to be satisfied for very long will eventually gain a reputation for being "spacy" or flighty or a loner. Third, and perhaps most important from the standpoint of social organization, the relatively free experimentation to which mating is subjected produces a quasi-band made up on the one hand of mated pairs and on the other hand of potential eligibles. After the process of experimentation has produced several different combinations of pairs, an air of intimacy pervades the quasi-band. And it is not uncommon for all the males and females in a group to have had intimate relations with each other. This represents to ghetto residents a "complete and total interaction with everyone you care about." But it also represents a potential source of friction: intimacy is everywhere a double-edged sword. Thus, if a couple decides to discontinue a relationship and breaks it off at some point there always exists the possibility that some former relationship will be revived by one or both of them. This is, of course, a threat to other member couples of the quasi-band and to the solidarity of the group. Such an event usually causes a temporary halt to the activities of the group until some new steady state is reached—often after couples have been realigned. In one instance a quasi-band consisting of several mated couples was thus endangered by the separation of one of the pairs. Over a two-week period interaction among members all but ceased until it was discovered partners had been exchanged within the group. Associations were then resumed among the same group of people arranged differently with no loss of membership. This kind of resolution of the conflicts inherent in this system of male-female relations is, however, almost utopian and unique to the writer's experience. Another instance, which seemed to occur more frequently, involved experiments with relationships consisting of three individuals. On one occasion two of the persons were male and the other female. This experiment reached the stage of cohabitation in the same household—every effort apparently being made by the three to succeed in their venture. On another occasion a similar experiment was attempted by two females and a male. In neither case, however, was the venture successful and each resulted in a monogamous pair, with the extra mate dropping out of sight entirely. As in the first example, the associational group ceased to function until the situation was resolved. Apparently the situation involving three mates—although thought to be an exciting alternative—was so unfamiliar that there were few cues as to appropriate behavior and the stress was too great for interaction among old friends to take place.

The most common solution to the problems that come with the constantly shifting courtship and mating alliances is simply the realignment of mates and the ouster of individuals who are displaced by such a realignment. This invariably causes tension and conflict and, as always, such problems are submitted to discussion and dissection by the gossip of friends and acquaintances. The nightly rap session (see Chapter 4) comes to be focused upon such events and the groups affected gradually become cohesive once again, while the absent or former members are criticized if their behavior was distasteful and admired if their withdrawal was graceful. At this point elders play an important role through their comments on the behavior of individuals in the ghetto. Stories of some of the more notorious sexual affairs of the past are told and values and beliefs reaffirmed. And any student of human social behavior will recognize what is going on here. It is not really a discussion of correct behavior or an impartial evaluation of the actions of the persons involved. Rather, what occurs after such a disturbance of the group's patterns of social interaction is a reassertion of the validity of that interaction pattern—a "rite of intensification" (Chapple and Coon 1942:507), in which all the remaining members of the group assert their rights to membership by declaring their loyalty, affirming the ideals of their fellows, and participating in ritualized gossip. In this way group life is preserved, and the individual who is not present can well afford to be denigrated for the good of those who remain members of the group. The individual is sacrificed to the end of maintaining customary patterns of interaction. A content analysis of the beliefs and ideals expressed in such a rite of intensification might reveal that certain themes—certain ideals even—are consistently expressed. One then might conclude that behavior is being judged against some kind of moral standard, but this would be putting the cart before the horse. An example will perhaps clarify what is meant.

In one quasi-band of elders and neophytes, males and females, the following event disturbed the interaction patterns of the group. Susan, the wife of John, traveled to another state with a male named Roy for the purpose of attending a rock festival. John found it necessary to remain in University City, since he had to work that particular weekend. Yet he expressed approval of Susan's plan to go anyway. At the conclusion of the excursion John discovered through the gossip of some of his friends and members of his quasi-band that Susan had made love with Roy over the weekend and, moreover, continued the affair during the following week. John then made it known to Susan and to the other members of the quasi-band that he wanted a separation. Susan's behavior was apparently unacceptable to him. Susan did not challenge John's decision and soon moved into Roy's apartment. During the evenings that followed the discussion topics often centered on Susan's behavior, and she was roundly condemned as "spacy" and "immature." John of course agreed with these pronouncements of the elders of the group and offered his own opinions on the nature of fidelity and the importance of loyalty and mutual trust between mates. In short, certain ideals were very definitely stated and applied to Susan's behavior and she was found wanting. Everyone agreed that Susan "has a bad head." One might conclude simply on the basis of a content analysis of symbolic communication that the ideals of loyalty, mutual trust, and fidelity were very important to members of this group. That is, people that were promiscuous were labeled by this group as "spacy," "immature," and "bad heads." Such a conclusion, however, would overlook the obvious facts that Roy had never been a member of this group, that Susan had left the group, and that John had remained. Obviously, the group members and particularly the elders would support John and condemn Susan and Roy in order to preserve the solidarity of the group. They could ill afford to support Roy and Susan, since they were not group members. This point is made even more clear when events of the succeeding months are examined.

After Susan left the group, John was unattached and began inviting females over in the evening. And gradually some of these came to be known by other group members. But John did not find another mate immediately after Susan's affair with Roy began. Susan continued to live with Roy, and John contemplated a divorce. About this time, two months later, Diane and Mike moved into the ghetto and came into contact with John's quasi-band. Like the other members of the quasi-band, Diane and Mike worked at the medical center—Diane as a secretary and Mike as a student in medical sociology. During the weeks that followed a strong affair developed between Diane and John. Diane lived with Mike, but they were not married. She apparently found John to be a better prospect and soon left Mike, becoming a member of John's quasi-band. Mike got quite angry and at one point challenged John and attempted to force a fight. John would not fight. Eventually Mike moved away, since Diane's liaison with John had been accepted by the quasi-band. Mike found the situation intolerable. During the discussions which followed these events Mike necessarily had to be sacrificed, and the reasons suggested by members of the group were that Mike was "hung up on status seeking" and that he had "straight ideas about loyalty." Diane often proclaimed that she liked Mike and wanted to continue to see him, but that he was too "hung up" and too "straight."

One will note that the behavior of Susan, John's former mate, and of Diane was almost exactly the same. One difference is that Susan left town and carried on her affair a little more discreetly. But the critical difference—and the point here—is that the rites of intensification conducted by the quasi-band approved the behavior of members of the group and condemned the behavior of those who found it necessary to leave the group. And in the two cases the ideals and beliefs paraded before the assembled members were in contradiction. Thus, the importance of the ritual is not the internal consistency of stated ideals and beliefs, but the preservation of social interaction among members of the group. To this end Susan and Roy and later Mike could easily be sacrificed. Later, perhaps, after the solidarity of the group had been assured the inconsistencies could be worked out. As it was, Diane eventually offered the clarification herself. Several weeks after Mike left the ghetto she mentioned that she preferred John because he had a regular job and obviously wanted to settle down and "begin living a normal life"; whereas Mike, being "hung up on status seeking," still wanted to earn his master's degree. Apparently she had grown tired of the impoverished life-style of a graduate student such as Mike. Eventually, she and John married and began living "a normal life."

This discussion of the dynamics of male-female relationships in the ghetto is a digression, but an important one to which we will refer later. But now let us pick up our hypothetical neophyte once again. We have seen him move through a period of socialization by means of the elder-neophyte pair relationship into a male-female relationship. It was said at the outset of this section that these two relationships are the building blocks of the hippie ghetto social organization, yet constant reference has been made to the importance of the quasi-band. At this point we will see that our neophyte has become a member of a much larger social network made up of such groups, and we will examine the final stage of the process in which our neophyte has engaged himself.

The neophyte, it has been pointed out, becomes a member of the ghetto social network by virtue of his participation in an elder-neophyte relationship. It is only through such a relationship that the neophyte can become socialized in the customs and beliefs of the ghetto society. We have already seen exactly how this is done; but now it is important to emphasize that the elder is a member of a quasi-band usually organized around a common means of subsistence. The neophyte becomes a member of this group if he finds the socialization process acceptable and desires to become affiliated. One does this by seeking to establish one's independence from his parents and by seeking to become dependent upon a quasi-band and its elders, who hold the keys to the important means of subsistence. It must be stressed, however, that the pair relationship is what makes membership in a quasi-band possible. We have seen how this operates with regard to male-female, or sexual, relationships; the same applies to the elder-neophyte realtionship. The neophyte who comes to dislike the nightly rites of intensification and the concomitant drug rituals will find himself ostracized by the group. Or the neophyte who independently finds a source of subsistence without the aid and approval of the elder will find himself suspect. For the elder-neophyte relationship persists for quite a long time—as long as the elder is present in the ghetto. He represents the tangible link between the neophyte and the subcultural world that lies beyond the ghetto. And maintenance of his vital link is important to the neophyte, for the final stage of life in the ghetto is the passage into the hippie subculture.

SUBCULTURES

Entrance into the subculture is marked by exit from the ghetto. One joins by moving away from the ghetto, together with his mate or alone if mate seeking has been unsuccessful or short-lived. But the term "subculture" should not be used, for there are many. It is more accurate to speak of *subcultures*. These hippie subcultures correspond almost exactly to the subsistence-related quasi-bands already discussed. The means of subsistence secured as part of the indoctrination process of the first stage of ghetto life can lead to other jobs, perhaps in other cities. And it is at this point that the traditional lore of the quasi-band, passed on to the neophyte from the elder, plays an important part in the lives of hippies. For this traditional knowledge—which initially appeared in the form of stories, conversations, and asides in the context of the nightly rap session—now links the ghetto resident to a network of former ghetto residents. The network may stretch to Canada and Europe and South America; it takes in New York, Boston, San Francisco, Los Angeles, Atlanta, Denver, Chicago, Miami, and other cities. And in all these places the ghetto resident will be able to contact people who may be able to assist him.

More importantly, the network offers the resident an identity and social position in his journey out of the ghetto and into a particular subculture. And in each subculture he will find people who know of hippie ghettos—often the one in University City—although they may never have been residents there. These new people may be from other cities and other scenes. What they and the ghetto resident have in common is friendship with the elders, who have gone before. In the subculture the ghetto resident will discover that the legendary ancestors actually exist, and he will draw support from them. If he is a member of a quasi-band involved in the drug traffic he will find persons in many towns and cities who can provide him with a place to live, contacts for cheap drugs, and perhaps a market. If he associated himself with those who formed the group that marketed the trappings of the hippie movement such as jewelry, water pipes, posters, and so on, he will find persons in other cities involved in the same activity. Similar contacts will be found by the group attached to the university, the group that made music on electric guitars, the group that studied architecture, the group that formed an agricultural commune, and so on. When members of these groups in University City leave the ghetto they find that many like themselves are engaged in the search for alternatives to straight society; and through the elder-neophyte and male-female relationships, they are able to find drug dealers, rock bands, communes, or whatever life in the ghetto has prepared them for.

A free school which has been started by the members of one quasi-band is an example of the kinds of alternatives to the larger society sought by residents of the hippie ghetto. This particular group is renovating an old house in a section of University City which was once prosperous but which in recent years has become rental property. The members of the group live in the house and work during the day at State University. In the evening they plan and prepare for the school. They envision a variety of classes, composed of students of all ages studying "whatever they are interested in." Members of the quasi-band feel that opportunities for the exchange of ideas and information between different age groups in American society have become alarmingly scarce, and they hope to promote an atmosphere of communication between the generations in their school. When asked how the staff of the school was to be recruited, the reply was that everyone would be volunteering his time and skills and no one connected with the school would be paid a salary. Many of the members of this quasi-band are from a university in the Midwest, and found their way to University City through the subcultural networks linking the ghetto to similar communities. They came to University City on the advice of friends who knew the town and its people.

The move out of the ghetto may be sparked by any number of circumstances, notably, as a response to the fluctuating opportunities in University City. Relocation may take place at almost any time, but, as already mentioned, it tends to occur most frequently in response to changes in the university calendar. The communication networks which exist between members of subcultural groups in different cities also play an important part, for they are extensive and at time pass on information with great rapidity. Thus, the hiring policy of Freedom Cable Television, Inc., sparked a minor migration to University City. The information was communicated through a network of travelers: in this case, two drug dealers who notified other dealers who in turn notified friends in different cities played an important role. On another occasion, when several people were making plans to start a commune in University City, word of this plan reached California via a traveler within two weeks. A member of that subcultural network who had been a former resident of the ghetto relayed word back that he was interested and would help buy the needed land and housing. But the commune never materialized and the California "relative" never appeared.

Those involved in the drug traffic are the most mobile of all ghetto residents; and their wide-ranging contacts throughout various subcultural groups make them prime vehicles for information and news. It was mentioned earlier that this observer had difficulty tracing such networks, since all phases of the study were carried out in University City. Knowledge about the actual workings of the drug network is lacking, but it can be inferred. In the winter of 1968, for example, a former ghetto resident who since relocating seven years previously had lived in Mexico, California, New York, and New Mexico spent one evening, from about six o'clock until nearly closing time, at the bar across the street from the ghetto. The observer happened to be present that evening and sitting with someone whose name the traveler had. The stranger's name turned out to be Howard and he had the observer's drinking companion's name written on a piece of paper. He located us by asking the bartender if so-and-so was in that night. When the bartender pointed out the person in question the traveler came over to the table and introduced himself. He had never met either the observer or his friend, yet through an elaborate process of "kinship-reckoning" he was able to establish his relationship with two total strangers. Moreover, he was able to demonstrate that he was part of a particular subcultural network as he spent several hours relating his adventures, telling stories about mutual friends, and relaying a host of information to the observer's drinking companion about people who had long since faded into ghetto legends. After nearly eight hours of stories that linked himself to his listeners, he cheerfully invited them to his camper to meet his wife, who had not accompanied him. When questioned about this he explained that she was a "Big Sur woman [who was] into a whole different trip than University City people." By this he meant that she would have little interest in the myriad stories of the evening, coming as she did from another subcultural group with its own quite different heritage.

Such travelers and the networks they represent symbolize to the resident of the hippie ghetto in University City an opportunity to establish relationships and forge important personal ties by which to survive as he himself travels. As mentioned before, the grapevine presents many such opportunities to ghetto residents who are ambitious enough to take them. In one sense, the whole social process of living in the hippie ghetto is pointed toward this subcultural stage. It is in the quasi-band networks developed in the ghetto that we see the development of the greatest number of alternatives opened to the neophyte and the greatest security in terms of his placement in a stable social system offered. In Chapter 6 we will return to his interpretation of hippie ghetto life and phrase it in a more traditional anthropological terminology, already introduced in this analysis, as a rite of passage. For now it is important only to emphasize that ghetto life has a characteristic social organization and that this social organization of the hippie ghetto, like the social organization of any other human grouping, grows out of certain social processes. The processes seen by this observer to be of most importance to hippies are the struggle for subsistence, mate seeking, and the transition from adolescence to adulthood. Yet at this point we have only touched the surface of the mechanics of social organization, pointing out the importance of pair relationships and the centrality of quasi-bands in ghetto life. We have not yet seen how the process actually works—how the elder becomes an important influence on the neophyte's decision, how the quasi-band can exert its power to sanction the behavior of its members and to preserve its membership. In order to do this we must consider the activities in which residents of the ghetto engage themselves. Then the functioning of the social organization sketched in this chapter will be better understood, for it is in regular and recurrent activities that the central features of hippie ghetto life are given both concrete and symbolic expression.

4 / The activities

RITUAL AND SOCIAL ORGANIZATION

The extent to which hippies are alienated from modern American society is a question of some importance. Hippies are disconnected from the larger society in a physical, psychological, and social sense. This much can be inferred simply from the brief references to the values and beliefs of hippies in the discussion of social organization in Chapter 3. Now we turn to the activities of hippie ghetto life that occur regularly—activities that give meaning and significance to ghetto life and activities that serve to articulate the structures discussed previously. The nature of these recurrent activities suggests the extent to which hippies can be considered alienated or estranged from American society. And an examination of the function and meaning of these activities indicates how the ghetto social system works.

We noted previously that ghetto residents must choose to enter the social network of hippie society and submit voluntarily to the process of socialization. But another question may be asked of this act of separation. How do hippies remain separated? A partial answer is to be found in the continual rejection and condemnation to which they are subjected at the hands of the larger society. Newspapers and magazines exploit their alleged decadence and editorialize for repression (*Reader's Digest* contains a choice example cited earlier). The American Medical Association (1966:658) has pronounced hippies to be pathogenic. Local community and state public officials emphasize the dangers of drugs and the deviant, criminal status of drug users. The man on the street—at least on the streets of University City—merely screams out of a car window, "Get a haircut. . . . Take a bath." The name used by the residents to identify their own neighborhood, "the ghetto," communicates most effectively the depth of their withdrawal from the onslaught.

But withdrawal and estrangement are not wholly explained in terms of repressive actions by outsiders. The remainder of the explanation is the response of ghetto residents to interaction with the larger society. Hippies engage in acts they know will draw condemnatory attention, as if they cannot afford to have their protest go unnoticed. In pursuing this point we would do well to borrow one of Goffman's (1961:148) ideas and note that the behavior of any group of people who are participants in a "total institution"[1] such as a school, asylum, military camp, or

---

[1] A total institution is one in which all life is structured by the demands of participation in that institution.

jail cannot be understood simply by examining interaction between teachers and students, keepers and inmates, officers and enlisted men, or guards and prisoners. Rather, participants in total institutions evolve among themselves systems of social organization in response to these formal and official patterns of interaction, so that much of the lives of inmates or students or prisoners or servicemen goes on independently of the administrative policy or keepers. To paraphrase Goffman, hippie behavior must be understood not only in terms of interaction with straight society but more importantly as a product of the social arrangements that evolve among hippies in response to straight society. These hip social arrangements are best understood through examination of the mechanism by which they are expressed. This mechanism dramatically punctuates hippie ghetto life. It is the ritual that has been called the "rap session"—the regular and recurrent ritual that is the central activity of the quasi-band.

It is in such ritual behavior that the anthropologist seeks to comprehend society as "a system of meaningful acts commonly shared" (Warner 1959:452). American anthropologists in particular have convincingly stressed the significance of the collective symbolic behavior expressed through the collective actions of a group in understanding the nature of that group (Chapple and Coon 1942:507; Kimball and McClellan 1966:244; Warner 1959:450). So it is with the intent of describing the more central realities of hippie ghetto life that we now present a detailed examination of the ritual behavior of hippies. The ritual residents of the ghetto call a rap session is, of course, not the only ritual event in their lives. But it is the most frequent ritual behavior and is characteristic of all the quasi-bands that make up ghetto society. And being the most frequent ritual activity—since it occurs practically nightly—the rap session is probably the most important, for the frequency of ritualized interaction is a clue to the importance of the symbols expressed in interaction in the lives of members of a group (Chapple and Coon 1942:398). Other rituals include the occasional festivals and celebrations to which some residents journey. These are peripheral to the ghetto, although those who attend the great festivals return with news and personal experiences. But even this kind of experience, or, rather, the process of recounting it to one's fellows, is ritualized within the context of a rap session.

THE "RAP SESSION"

The significance of ritualized communication between members of a quasi-band is stressed by the label applied to the ritual: "to rap" means to establish rapport, to converse in a meaningful manner, to talk truthfully and honestly. In such behavior one can catch a glimpse of the extreme isolation and estrangement of ghetto residents. The separation of ghetto residents from the larger society is much more than mere physical isolation. For example, newspapers are rarely found in a ghetto apartment. Televisions and radios are scarce; and news broadcasts are simply unimportant. Magazines and new periodicals, though more common than newspapers, are still relatively scarce. Almost no one subscribes to underground literature, although some residents may purchase current issues at the head shop downtown.

The points here are that straight society is to be distrusted and, that the concerns of straights are not usually the concerns of hippies. Information from the outside world is irrelevant to life in the ghetto, except as it relates to the experiences of residents. Thus, the major source of relevant information is the resident's own personal experience. Rapping with one's fellows is considered the best of all possible ways to gain a clear view of the world, undistorted by the mediating functions of distrusted editors, politicians, and the like. Story telling is obviously a well-developed skill among hippie ghetto residents, functioning as it does to build traditions, indoctrinate initiates, and communicate information.

This is not to say there are no other sources of information. Books of fiction and poetry, and records are considered highly credible sources. The usefulness of such books is rather easy to understand. An author of a lengthy novel creates a total impression of his viewpoint, or the realities of the world as he sees them, as opposed to the journalist, who fragments the world and studiously avoids comprehensive, integrated projections of his own views. An author of a novel reveals himself—his fantasies, distortions, and illusions—in his writing. The reader may judge the validity of an interpretation of the world more easily if the author is subjective, for as the reader comes to know the writer he comes to understand the sources of bias and insight, perspective and interpretation. In short, the novel is credible because the *reader* judges credibility. The songs that fill the ghetto every evening are more than simple entertainment. They too are considered credible sources of information, for the performer augments lyrical messages with other kinds of communication, which when taken together inform the listener and involve him in the totality of a given experience, mood, or tale. The validity of the words and mood created is once again judged by the individual.

There is probably no better example of a rite of intensification (Chapple and Coon 1942:507) in ghetto life than the rap session, although there are others whose effects are not as general such as invitations to dinner, visiting, and sexual intercourse. The rite of intensification occurs in the evening, usually after residents return to the ghetto after a day of "coping with straights." Life in the straight world is taxing and always a source of pain to residents; the evening brings the balm of companionship, shared experiences, and rededication to the spirit of how life ought to be. When the quasi-band members gather they are often invited to choose music for the drug ceremony. Music is felt to be an important aid in establishing rapport, as is the commonly shared drug experience, for they are both group experiences. This point deserves further elaboration, otherwise drug use might be thought of as an individual act—something one person does to himself and that affects only him. There could be no more inaccurate portrayal of the role of drugs in the hippie ghetto.

MARIJUANA

The evening ritual begins with the passing of a joint, each person in succession drawing the marijuana smoke deeply into his lungs, holding it there, and passing the joint to the next person. Marijuana, smoked either in cigarette form or in a

Some of the common ritual items include a water pipe, an ounce of marijuana, and cigarette papers. (Photo by Nancy Sterngold)

pipe, is the drug of choice among hippies in University City. LSD, peyote, mescaline, psilocybin, amphetamines, barbiturates, and cocaine are not used with anything approaching regularity. The use of these drugs becomes widespread in the ghetto only when a shipment arrives. Given the fact that they were difficult to obtain during the period of study, they did not enjoy the universality or centrality that marijuana did. Heroin, morphine, alcohol, and other addictive drugs are readily available in the ghetto and certain groups use them habitually, but data on these groups are lacking for reasons already indicated. Returning to the drug of choice —marijuana—one is tempted to engage in the dialogue among physicians, politicians, journalists, police officials, the courts, and parents regarding the actual, potential, or suspected effects of the drug upon the individual and society. But that argument is a morass into which the anthropologist need not venture, for our purpose here is not to examine the effects of drugs upon the mind of the user but to examine the ways in which the drug is used. Still, it is curious to note that *Cannabis sativa* is one of man's oldest and most widely used drugs and that, contrary to popular belief, *much* is known about its use (Subcommittee on Alcoholism and Narcotics 1971:53). Marijuana is not new to North America and enjoyed widespread medical and therapeutic use up until the passage of the Marijuana Tax Act in 1937. At that time the drug was contained in twenty-eight preparations marketed to the public. The Subcommittee on Alcoholism and Narcotics (1971: 53–54) lists the following among the ailments for which marijuana was used: excessive menstrual cramps and bleeding, treatment and prophylaxis of migraine headaches, alleviation of withdrawal symptoms of opium and chloral hydrate addiction, tetanus, insomnia, delirium tremens, muscle spasms, strychnine poisoning, asthma, cholera, dysentery, labor pains, psychosis, spasmatic cough, excess anxiety, gastrointestinal cramps, depression, nervous tremors, bladder irritation, and psychosomatic illness. Nor is belief in the medical and therapeutic effectiveness of marijuana unique to American culture. The plant has been used in medical preparations for about five thousand years.

Hollister (1971) in a recent summary of research with marijuana observed that the current resurgence of use of marijuana has stimulated an increase in scientific interest in the effects of the drug. Yet present research may have added very little that was not already known. One reason for this is that the production of synthetic tetrahydrocannabinol (THC), believed to be the chemically active intoxicant contained in *Cannabis sativa*, has only become possible in the last ten years. Not until the late 1950s were pharmacological studies that provided some degree of precision possible. And the pharmacological properties of the drug are still unknown due to difficulties of administration in precise quantities by the smoking technique and due to the fact that quantitative evaluation of THC action in the human body is unavailable, since it is not yet certain that THC is the major or only active ingredient. Studies of the physiological effects of the drug indicate no changes in pupil size, respiratory rate, deep tendon reflexes, or temperature, although all observers report increases in pulse rate as well as reddening of the eyes. The perceptual and psychic change reported most frequently is euphoria, especially among students and less so among imprisoned former drug addicts. Sleepiness was constantly observed, time sense altered, hearing less discriminant, and vision reportedly sharper with many visual distortions. Depersonalization and difficulty with thinking were common observations. Several studies have reported the impairment of serial addition, freehand drawing, and sequential thought which suggest interference with decision making and short-term memory processes.

While the studies reviewed by Hollister (1971) are all clinical in nature, he notes quite properly that the signs and symptoms delineated in the laboratory correlate well with those reported in social use. Certainly, the characteristics reported above are fully in agreement with those described by residents of the ghetto and observed by this writer. And ghetto residents would agree with the numerous studies that have pointed to psychological dependence (physical dependency is unknown), although these informants would hastily enumerate alcohol, nicotine, and caffeine as socially acceptable drugs that also produce psychological dependency. Ghetto residents would view the other reported negative effects of marijuana —personality change, loss of desire to work, loss of motivation, and impairment of judgment and intellectual functions—not as inherently destructive, but as "negative" only in terms of the social prejudices held by the larger society. In fact, they feel that personality change is often beneficial; loss of motivation is acceptable and may stem from a desire to avoid participation in an evil society bent on economic and military domination; and the alteration of intellectual functions present the individual with further opportunity to explore and experiment with alternative ways of thinking. As Hollister (1971) points out, questions such as these—which involve peoples' values—are not answerable merely by laboratory and clinical experiments. Yet these questions must be answered if the legal, social, and medical regulations on marijuana are to be rational and equitable. In short, science is not likely to discover in the very near future solutions to such social problems. In the absence of objective data, then, advocates and critics of the use of marijuana will probably continue to engage in the human penchant for debate and discussion.

Given man's historical familarity with marijuana the current debate over its legality, harmfulness, and chronic effects becomes even more interesting. As Wallace (1959) points out, the effects of marijuana vary with the cultural and social setting in which the drug is used. Like peyote, mescaline, and other substances that produce hallucinatory effects, the content, interpretation, and meaning of the effects are a matter of the hallucinator's response to the experience. And this will be determined by current beliefs and cultural traditions which the user has learned as a member of a social group. The Ponca or Menomini Indian (Spindler and Spindler, 1971) who ingests a hallucinatory substance expects and experiences something quite different than does the jazz musician in New Orleans or the college freshman. And, more significantly, the act of ingesting such a substance carries different meanings in different cultures. In American culture hippies have called the drug experience a "trip" and interpret the effects of psychedelic drug use as a journey toward maturation and spiritual growth (Wallace, 1969). As Davis and Munoz (1968:160) discovered in San Francisco, a "good head" is someone who uses drugs for the purposes of self-discovery, greater awareness, and spiritual learning. And as Wallace (1969) mentions, this interpretation of a quest or search is part of our cultural tradition, a cultural form which is very old in Western civilization and vividly expressed in John Bunyan's *Pilgrim's Progress*. Given the cultural context in which such drugs have grown in popularity, namely, during the period of transition from adolescence to adulthood, Wallace's argument becomes all the more compelling.

In the 1960s several observers commented upon the Western religious symbolism employed by hippies (Berger 1967; Keniston 1960). And it is not surprising to note the way in which the so-called hippie movement has dovetailed into the many religious cults which have become popular in the 1970s. Nor is it difficult to understand what is happening when freaks, hippies, or heads mass in Shea Stadium to hear evangelist Billy Graham. The proliferation of "Jesus freaks" is welcomed in many quarters of straight society, and some may even feel that such renewed interest in the Judeo-Christian tradition is a healthy sign; but few like to have it pointed out that the midwife of this revival is a drug-induced state of euphoria. While it may be something of an overstatement to draw parallels between Bunyan's heroic Pilgrim and the adolescents sitting in a circle smoking pot and listening to the Rolling Stones, it is a theme to which we will return later.

Now let us turn to our quasi-band as it gathers together for the rite of intensification. The ritual is begun by passing the marijuana from person to person. Even when there is an abundance of grass, people follow this pattern of communally sharing the sacramental substance. After each individual receives the cigarette or pipe, inhales deeply, and passes it on to the next person, he leans back and concentrates upon retaining the smoke. It is felt that this action heightens the effects of smoking. One person after another emits satisfied groans, muffled comments, or simply smiles of approval. Thus as the sacrament travels around the room a slow cadence is set up by the participants' sounds and gestures of approval and satisfaction. This cadence does not seem to be entirely a function of the individual-specific effects of the intoxicant. Becker (1963:46–48) has outlined the procedure through which one learns the technique of smoking marijuana in order to get high. And unless the participant has smoked tobacco before, it is a difficult task to inhale the marijuana smoke and hold it in the lungs. Many persons in the group studied in University City reported having such difficulty when first learning the technique. But one does not simply get high. One must also learn to perceive the effects of marijuana (Becker 1963:48–53) and to enjoy or at least feel relaxed with the perceptual distortions that occur (Becker 1963:53–58). Again, many informants indicated that they had difficulty getting high the first several times they smoked the drug. Only through continued practice were they able to become aware of perceptual distortions, mood changes, and altered mental functions. One male reported smoking five joints with an elder before noticing anything unusual. And these observations have been duplicated in clinical research. Weil, Zinberg, and Nelsen (1968:1240–1242) report that naive subjects who were given marijuana in both low and high doses did not experience strong subjective experiences, and the effects they did perceive are different from those described by regular users given the same amounts in the same setting. The points to be made, then, are that marijuana use in the ghetto is not an individual act and its most important effects are not individual-specific. The social atmosphere created in the drug ritual is what acts to interpret the individual-specific effects of the drug and translate them into group phenomena.

To take part in a rap session is to join others in seeking rapport, which is characterized by residents as a shared psychic state that is at once personal and consensual. For, as we have seen, the marijuana high is largely a product of the actions of others. A sociologist (Winick 1959–1960:244) discovered that jazz musicians used the term "contact high" to describe a "special kind of emotional group contagion" which is picked up by a nondrug-using member of a musical group that performs while using marijuana. This "emotional group contagion" is well recognized by residents of the ghetto, who call it a "contact high" as well as "good vibrations" and simply "grooving." References to this rapport which can be induced in the drug ritual are common. An informant says:

> You know when you're really grooving together. You know what each other is thinking. Sometimes you can just look in his eyes and just break into a grin. No words . . . words aren't needed when you're getting good vibes . . . it's where it's at, getting close to people.

The wholehearted enthusiasm with which hippies greet such intimate feelings is predicated on an assumption that others are more honest, more open, and more themselves while intoxicated on marijuana than they are normally. The logic behind such an assumption can be inferred from the widely reported fact that marijuana seems to produce a feeling of adequacy, well-being, and euphoria in addition to a contact high among users (Hollister 1971). It is widely felt by ghetto residents that inhibitions are shed by a person under the influence of marijuana. In one instance a resident was introducing marijuana to his new brother-in-law. The initiate was at first cautious and suspicious. As the evening wore on and more of the drug was consumed, the resident discovered that the initiate was interested in cameras and turned the conversation to photography. The initiate, who had previously not stirred from his chair, promptly fetched his newest camera and began lecturing without stopping for about five minutes while looking most of the time at his prized possession. When he paused as if to answer questions, he apparently realized his outburst was uncharacteristic and apologized. The ghetto resident assured him, "That happens when you're stoned."

Whether or not people are indeed more honest, less inhibited, or more themselves while smoking pot is beside the point. It is enough that ghetto residents believe this to be the case, for this belief tends to dictate their attitude toward the drug and influence their perception while under its influence. The residents often revel in outbursts of uninhibited behavior even if it is hostile because they feel that the actor (and the audience) learns something of himself from such outbursts —something that he might not normally see. An extreme example of this belief in the efficacy of drug use for learning about one's hidden self occurred when a visitor in the ghetto unsuccessfully attempted to seduce his host's mate. The visitor's frustration was apparent when he began alternately threatening and then moaning, being aggressive and then withdrawn. Rather than confronting the offensive individual, the host remained calm and attempted to quiet the visitor's fears that he had offended. Witnesses later described the behavior of the visitor as "beautiful" because "that's really what Steve is like. . . . That's his hangup." They felt that Steve had learned something from his attempted seduction, and that fact was more important than the offense to the host.

Just as the loss of inhibitions and the achievement of a shared psychic state are felt to be products of the rap session, insight is felt to be achieved by ritualized drug use. The world is quite different when one is high. Residents feel they are able to concentrate better and see more clearly because they discover things in the rap session. As conversation progresses it is not uncommon for participants in the ritual to offer their insights for the consideration of the group. And it is not uncommon for such offerings to call forth pronouncements from the elders of the group. A long story about his experiences in the Highland County jail was related by a resident one evening. The speaker told of establishing rapport with the other prisoners and feeling very good towards them. One of the elders of the group broke in with:

> That's it man . . . when you're in jail you're all alike, in the same place. Like, there's no point hassling and that's beautiful. Spades, red-necks . . . like, we're all the same.

The drug marijuana, which is always used in the rap session, obviously has effects independent of the social context in which it is used. But the facts that response to the drug is a function of group action; that techniques of smoking, perception of the effects, and enjoyment of the effects must all be learned; and that the meaning of the act and of the things perceived while using the drug are dictated by cultural beliefs and traditions, emphasize the significance of the ritualization of drug use among ghetto residents. As noted above, ritualization produces a specific psychic state called rapport. And the fact that ghetto residents rarely smoke alone reinforces the idea that there is much more to smoking marijuana than the individual high. The ritualization of the act draws people into close, intimate patterns of interaction. As any businessman who wants to close a deal over a drink can testify, intoxication is often used to lubricate the social machinery. The alleged property of the drug to break down inhibitions, and thus reveal the "true" nature of personality makes intimate interaction all the more meaningful for those who believe passionately in being "themselves." The sharing of insights about the nature of the world offers the group the opportunity to affirm again and again its solidarity and, therefore, the rightness of its actions.

It seems reasonable, then, that participation in the rap session and the drug ceremony which is an integral part of it is not completely a matter of individual motivation. Motivation to participate is supplied by the quasi-band. When the sacrament is passed and refused, the offending person is usually asked "What's the matter?" or "Are you uptight about something tonight?" It is important that everyone present participate in the ritual, probably because of the central importance to the group of achieving the shared psychic state. The ritual cannot be properly conducted if some people present are "down" or "on a bummer." While a person on a bummer is not usually ejected from the gathering, he is questioned in a way that indicates to him and to all others present that his behavior is irregular and out of order. For the act of smoking marijuana is a collective act. Returning to Warner's (1959:452) emphasis upon "meaningful acts commonly shared," we may define the ghetto society by such collective behavior. Not to participate in the nightly rap session is not to be a member of ghetto society.

There is still another, more transparent, explanation of the obligatory nature of participation in the rap session. Possession of marijuana is illegal, and all participants in the ritual are technically criminals. It is widely recognized that drug users, bohemians, homosexuals, jazz musicians, career criminals, and deviant subcultures in general develop hostilities and counterstigmas directed towards outsiders (Davis 1967:160; Polsky 1967:65). For hippies, "straights" is such a pejorative term. It is used to describe those who fear the effects of drugs, do not trust themselves under the influence of drugs, or for some other reason do not use drugs. This explanation of the rap session, however, is too categorical to be of much use. For the use of drugs, as should be apparent by now, has greater significance than simple we-they group dynamics.

Still, one should recognize that news media, state and federal legislative bodies, state and federal agencies, community civic groups, the American Medical Association, the American Pharmaceutical Association, the President of the United States, and the United Nations have emphasized continually the harmful effects of certain drugs and the deviant status of certain drug users. Not to consider this onslaught as contributing to the nature of the drug ritual would be simple-minded. For, after all, the following comment is not atypical of those groups opposed to the use of marijuana:

Beware! Young and Old—People in All Walks of Life! This [picture of a joint] may be handed you by the *friendly stranger*. It contains the Killer Drug "Marijuana"—a powerful narcotic in which lurks Murder! Insanity! Death! (Solomon 1966:497).

The poster quoted above hung on the walls of several ghetto apartments although its publishers, the Interstate Narcotic Association, Chicago, Illinois, recommends that it be hung in trains, buses, streetcars, and other public conveyances. The threat such propaganda campaigns represent to residents of the ghetto is real and well recognized, although almost everyone was amused and coveted the poster as an object of pop art. The rap sesssion, therefore, can be seen to stem in part from the felt need for group solidarity and the protection of group members. Drug use in the ritual can be seen to be both an important act of defiance and an important act of camaraderie.

RITUAL COMMUNICATION

Returning once again to the pattern of the social interaction in the ghetto, and dismissing momentarily the deviant aspects of that pattern, we see that the function of ritualized behavior becomes even more complex when we recall that a large body of traditional lore is maintained in this fashion. The initial ceremony of the rap sesssion which involves establishing a desired level of rapport through the use of drugs is a prelude—an achievement of setting and mood—for the ceremonial communication of information. Communication during the rap session is said to be ceremonial for two reasons: first, it is called "rapping"; second, it occurs after rapport has been established via the sharing of a sacrament. The stories told always involve the personal experience of one or more individuals present in the room or of some individual known to those present. Experiences of the day are interwoven with and may provide the stimulus for the many tales and anecdotes in a group's traditional body of lore.

In a very general sense, the tales accumulated by a quasi-band can be lumped into three categories: (1) those which relate good, or groovy, behavior towards straight society, (2) those which stress the dangers and hypocrisies of straight society, and (3) those which project alternatives to straight society. Examples of each of these are introduced below.

Tales which illustrate a desirable relationship with straight society are cast in a mold of the absurdity of life, which can be at once humorous and tragic. Hippies ridicule those who don't know "where it's at" because they are caught up in straight society's "games." Policemen, public officials, bureaucrats, radical students, and others who occupy positions in the formal institutions of straight society are favorite sources for such tales.

> . . . we were a pretty scruffy-looking group and we had the truck stuffed to the roof, so the customs officer decides we look suspicious and need to be searched. So his peon assistant starts taking it all out while he stands there looking official in his shining uniform pointing out all the things he wants us to open. We're helping the peon because we wanted to get out of there as soon as possible. But we were clean so we gave them a lot of hassle. Finally they drag out the footlocker with the turtle heads in it [the speaker collected them for the museum in University City]. They were starting to rot on the beach when we picked them up . . . When the official sees the footlocker he says, "Ah, what's in this?" And we said, "Oh, nothing. Just some specimens." Imagine this sort of low hum

coming from the footlocker. . . . The flies must have already laid their eggs in the heads, and by now there were millions of hatched maggots feeding on them. He told us to open it. We didn't give him any shit, we just said, "There's nothing in it but some old rotten turtle heads." Well, he tells the peon to open it up. They cracked it open and this huge cloud of flies engulfs the peon who goes running off screaming . . . and the stench takes the starch out of this cat's uniform.

Another tale pits the wit and presence of mind of the ghetto resident against the dull, rigid behavior of a straight attempting to enforce his will.

The car broke down halfway to Louisiana and the nearest city was Tyler, Texas. We didn't have any bread so I figured, go to a bank—that's where they keep the money, right? We go to a teller at the Tyler Texas National Bank and she sends us to the head cashier. This guy is really sad, man, and he sees us coming. I could see him asking himself, "What kind of fool is this?" I'm wearing boots and jeans and my Seminole jacket, haven't shaved in days. I told him I needed to cash a check, explained the whole car bit. He said he couldn't do it. I told him my bank in University City would guarantee it would be good, and he said, "Why, no bank in the world will do that. They might tell me you have the money in your account today but they won't guarantee payment on your check." . . . I finally convinced him to call my bank. Then he asked me who would pay for the call and I told him to charge it to my home phone. Now he was really uptight . . . [saying] "The phone company won't do that." I get really self-righteous and tell him to try it to see if it worked. . . . The operator placed the call, and his mouth dropped open. While we were waiting he tried to be friendly and make polite conversation. "What do you do?" I told him I was a psychologist [the speaker was not a psychologist] and he freaked out; all of a sudden he starts treating me nice, asking questions about complexes and interesting this and interesting that. Then he got the bank and asked about the check and they said they would guarantee it. Then his mouth really dropped open and he began apologizing and asking more questions. He didn't know who I was but he thought he had offended me and apologized about six times as I walked to the door; he'd been wrong and nasty to boot, so he was really freaking out.

Still other tales which stress groovy behavior relate to the institutions of straight society, but not specifically to individuals who occupy positions of authority. A favorite target is the military, and several stories grew out of the experiences of those who took part in the massive march on the Pentagon in the fall of 1967.

When we got up near the top of the hill there were troops chasing people away from the side doors. The activists were running around and then there was a break in the crowd—about two hundred feet—and the pacifists were all lined up cheering and shouting. Everyone was getting gassed, even if they weren't trying to break through to the doors. So Phil and I went around to the front ramps that lead up to the main doors and joined this mob trying to rush up the ramp. The troops were still at the top of the hill, so we just pushed slowly up the ramp. But before we got halfway up about twenty MPs jumped over the wall and started swinging into the front of the mob. Man, everybody panicked and turned around and split. But before we'd taken two steps people were yelling, "Cool it!" "Don't Run!" "Walk." So everybody stopped and walked slowly down the ramp. Nobody ran. The MPs kept doing their thing, wacking away at the back of the mob, but nobody ran. Like, it was beautiful. People with good heads, good enough to know that the war is bad, really can stop. . . . It's like they weren't a mob . . . they were all thinking, intelligent individuals.

The examples offered by ghetto residents of beautiful events which occurred at the Pentagon march are numerous. Some tell of hospitality, some of shared food, blankets, and whiskey to help ward off the cold wind that swept over those who chose to sit in all night on the Pentagon steps. One tale features a resident of the ghetto who, upon becoming enthusiastic at the rally which was held before the march, rolled his draft card around a joint and smoked it. The story goes that all his friends gathered and passed the joint around the circle which spontaneously formed. As others who were nearby saw this, they came over to join in, including some "middle-age straights" and an elderly woman. The ghetto resident claimed that he never got a second drag off his card because so many people joined the circle to participate in the symbolic act.

But not all of the stories related to groovy behavior explicitly state the character of such behavior; sometimes such ideals are implied by negative examples where behavior that is considered particularly "uncool" is ridiculed or condemned. A noteworthy example involves a group that journeyed to Oklahoma in the summer of 1967 to "visit the Indians."

> I should have known not to take her in the first place. When we were all sitting around the night before we left, grooving on what we were going to do and all, she said, "Gee, I've never made it with an Indian before." She and George weren't yet split up, but it was a bad scene anyway between them; but George encouraged her to go if she really wanted to. . . . We got in just before the dancing started Friday night and she wandered away. . . . Next time I saw her was after the main thing was over. She ran up and said she was with a great group of kids that were going to have an "after-the-dance-orgy." "Yeah, groovy." I tried to argue that all those people were juiced out of their minds—it might be a really bad scene. She said she would do her own thing. . . . I didn't want to be around all those drunks. . . . She did her thing until we got ready to split Sunday and went out to find her. . . . She had decided she had really found out where it was at and was going to stay and live with the Indians. Well, I thought, "That's cool, but what about George." We hassled her into calling him on the phone and telling him; and on the way to the phone we really hassled her about the Indians being poor and not needing some spaced-out white chick hanging around. Man, she was freaky. When we couldn't reach George, she decided she'd write him a note. And that hacked it right there. Like, we put her in the car and just drove right back to University City. She was really freaked out and didn't speak to anybody. She hated me and every time she started bitching I just hit her with her juice-head [one who consumes alcohol] Indian teeny-boppers [high-school age adolescents].

The second major category of tales emphasizes the dangers of living in straight society and in having any contact with straights. The hypocrisies seen in the straight world are felt to be a particularly unendurable source of danger for ghetto residents, so hypocrisy is a common theme of these tales. But the much more important themes relate to the very real threats hippie ghetto residents face from police, public officials, and parents.

> Bill scored some tea one time from the Coast when the town was dry. I mean really dry—people were hoarding little stashes in pill bottles. He mailed the bread out there and had this cat send the stuff to his mother's house in Jonestown, thinking that postal inspectors would open any package from San Francisco

addressed to University City and weighing about two pounds. It was a groovy plan except it didn't work. The ki [kilo] got to his mother's house before he got down there in time and she opened it. Well, she panicked and called the fuzz and they picked him up in University City . . . threw him in the Jonestown jail drunk tank . . . shaved his head and beat the shit out of him three or four times. His mother let him sit there for two days and then got him a lawyer. The lawyer told her that Bill was beaten and shaved and all that . . . and she freaked out again and went running down to the jail to get him out of there. Like, cops ain't supposed to do that, not in middle-class, normal Jonestown. And, man, the drag is that she did it for his own good, dig it?

This incident and several others like it attract wide attention in the ghetto. But the dangers a ghetto resident may face at the hands of hypocritical and helpful parents are even greater than arrest and rough treatment by the police. The son of a rather wealthy family was suspected by his parents of being addicted to heroin. His parents apparently had their suspicions validated when their son was arrested on charges of sale and possession of marijuana, for after he had posted bond with a lawyer, they showed up one morning for the ostensible purpose of working out the details of his case. Instead, the lawyer drew up commitment papers and the young man was incarcerated in an asylum.

As might be expected, the draft and the armed forces are viewed as dangerous threats emanating from straight society. Residents of the ghetto are a source of valuable information concerning escape from the draft. It is commonly stated that "any head can outsmart the freaks that sit on draft boards." Of course, he must be prepared to adopt illegitimate means in order to achieve this goal. Many residents use the technique of "freaking out," which simply means convincing an army psychologist or psychiatrist that they are insane. A creative imagination has little difficulty inventing such a facade, and a dedicated and/or skillful actor can carry it off. Drugs are a common aid if one wants to freak out at the draft physical.

John was up on acid for about four days before his physical and wandered into the place about two days after he was ordered to be there. He kind of wandered up to somebody and said he was there to be examined. . . . They looked him up and said, "You were supposed to be here day before yesterday." And John says, "That Ronnie's problem. He was supposed to get me here." So they sent him down to see the shrink after about an hour of this "That's Ronnie's problem." And John starts down the hall, but he never gets there. He starts talking to all these people and takes out his harmonica and plays for this sergeant that digs blues. And about four that afternoon he wanders back to the front desk and they go off again on why he never got to the shrink. Man, he says, he was so spaced out that they gave him a 1-Y without ever examining him.

Another ghetto resident cut off his little toe with a cold chisel just before his pre-induction physical. He thought that this act would qualify him for a psychological deferment, but when he got to his physical examination the army functionaries were not impressed.

I told this cat that I cut off my toe myself. And he didn't blink, just kept on asking me questions. Like, I was just being processed right on through and they weren't going to let me see the shrink. Finally, I felt like I could cry, so I did and started pleading and grabbing this guy by the shirt. Then he kind of yawned and sent me to the shrink's office. I had kept myself super uptight through the whole thing, you know, not talking to anyone or joking to let off the tensions and be more at ease. . . . I'd worn clothes that were too small, I was dirty, hadn't shaved. . . . When they sat me down to wait I never moved out of the desk, never took a leak or anything. But then when they finally called me, I got up and realized I was tired and kind of dragging, and that's bad, man. I want to be as hyper as possible. So I started thinking about taking a leak and about cutting off another toe if they passed me, and that put me up there again.

Tactics such as these and others such as drug addiction, homosexuality, and obscene tattoos are offered up during the rap session in the context of tales about people who have tried them. And, of course, escape to Canada through the necessary contacts in an "underground railroad" is always a very real alternative, and the mechanics of the procedure are all contained within the traditional lore of specific quasi-bands.

The third category of tales communicated in the rap session relates to alternatives to life in the straight world. These stories often take the form of projections or plans for some utopian solution to the pressures and dangers of straight life. Communal arrangements and experiments are perhaps the most frequent alternatives aired. One such alternative involved several former residents of the ghetto, who upon relocating became dissatisfied with living outside the ghetto and sought to establish a cooperative living arrangement. They searched for a house large enough to house four couples comfortably, but during the time they spent searching it became apparent that no one could really commit himself for a two-year period (all but one couple were students). The group felt that less than two years would not provide a long-enough time to test the validity of the experiment. But several features of the plan were agreed upon in the course of many nights of rapping about the co-op. First, each person would have his or her own room; that is, couples would not share rooms. Second, there would be a "communal room" where people might go to rap and socialize and which would also serve as a meeting room. In the course of planning, one of the members of this group told of a girl whom all the others had known who lived on a communal farm for two years in New York State. The New York commune members experienced tensions and conflicts soon after the venture became successful and new people began to appear. They resolved such tensions by holding "head sessions" in a tepee, wherein all of the members of the commune would assemble to work out its problems. No one was permitted to leave until a solution was reached; once such a session went on for thirty-six hours—until the problem was resolved when one of the members decided to leave the farm and the commune remained intact. The ghetto residents who hoped to start a co-op agreed that maintaining group unity would be a vital purpose of the communal room. In this same vein, it was widely known that a communal living arrangement on Hog Island failed when the group split into two factions and ceased meeting together, hence, did not iron out difficulties and eventually stopped cooperating. The theme of rap sessions for the purpose of resolving conflicts occurs in most of the suggested alternatives to straight society.

Another plan to create an alternative to straight society grew up among a group of artists and art students. Dissatisfied with the art department's emphasis upon art history and teaching art history, they sought a commune of artists, craftsmen, and artisans. They planned to obtain land in North Carolina where they might attract local craftsmen. Their plan was to buy forested land, sell the timber to a lumber company, and use the proceeds of the sale to construct cabins. Several members of the commune would have to live all year at the commune, in the winter marketing the products of the group in nearby cities. The remainder might then maintain their ties with universities, museums, and galleries in order to obtain operating capital. Few of the plans offered as alternatives to straight society are well grounded in the facts of straight society. The failure to take into account the logistics of a plan was illustrated when a group of travelers from California passed through the ghetto, stopping for several days to rest and gather converts. The group consisted of three females and two males, one of whom obviously played the role of organizer and spokesman. No converts were found in the hippie ghetto—probably because the group had little idea how it would achieve its goal. Its members knew only that they were seeking to create a feeling of "family" among themselves. The group's spokesman noted that achieving this feeling was almost impossible in this country; he had been in several communes on the West Coast and had never found it. Consequently, the group was seeking to establish a commune somewhere on an island off the coast of Florida. The members were headed for Miami and hoped to get more information there. The spokesman told his hosts in the hippie ghetto, "You are like a family here. I can tell that people aren't uptight with this place. It's like a head community, except that the city's a drag."

The reason that "the city's a drag" was implied in Chapter 3 on living and working together. It is difficult for freaky people to obtain jobs. But this statement that the city is a drag can also be interpreted as a generic reference to the fact that living in the city brings one into contact with many different kinds of people and situations. And for those seeking separation and isolation, moving out of the city is necessary. Such a move, it is thought, also tends to lessen conflicts and tensions between friends and associates. It is debatable whether more converts to the Florida venture were not found in the University City ghetto because the residents there had found a feeling of "family." A more accurate interpretation of the residents' reaction to this plan might be that they weren't necessarily satisfied with University City, but they were definitely unimpressed by an unknown island off the coast of Florida.

Besides communal living, other alternatives to straight society are offered for discussion in the rap session. One of the more popular is the Kerouac style of traveling between various hippie population centers, visiting a variety of scenes to get a sample of alternatives available, and embarking on adventures abroad, notably in Mexico and Europe. The ever-increasing flow of migrant adolescents through the ghetto stimulates the residents to make such plans. And like communes, traveling or living on the road is a kind of separation and felt to offer a potential for self-discovery and spiritual growth like that offered in a psychedelic trip. Alternatives to straight society, then, are modeled on the ghetto itself: a separate, isolated population knit together through ritual behavior and linked to other, similar populations through networks of goods, services, and "relatives."

THE PLACE OF RITUAL IN GHETTO LIFE

In summary, the rap session is a ritual in which the major features of ghetto life are reflected. The ritual can be divided into two parts: ceremonial drug use and ceremonial communication. The first part of the ritual serves to establish a mood in which all of the participants achieve a feeling of communal well-being. This mood is a shared psychic state in that participants believe it to be productive of a kind of rapport unavailable outside the context of the ritual. The drug itself is viewed as a vital and necessary stimulus for achieving the shared psychic state, yet the nature of the drug is such that appreciation of its effects—especially effects that might be shared with others—must be learned. So the body of beliefs and actions which accompany drug use are perhaps more crucial than the drug itself in the achievement of the shared psychic state. The belief that the drug is an aid to self-discovery implies that certain expectations regarding the drug experience may become self-fulfilling prophecies. In other words, people are expected to be more honest and more themselves when stoned, and this expectation may produce such behavior. The approval with which uninhibited and spontaneous acts are greeted serves to further reinforce such behavior. The ceremonial acts of sharing the sacrament, focusing attention on a shared experience such as listening to music or relating stories and gossip, and the cadence of exclamations expressing satisfaction all function to reinforce belief in the shared psychic state by helping to produce it. Thus, the first part of the ritual functions to set a mood for that which is to come.

The second part of the ritual, called rapping, is probably the more significant of the two ceremonies. The name of the ritual, "rap session," points to its importance; and the drug ceremony is very much a prelude to it. The central importance of this ceremony stems from the all-important ideals of self-fulfillment, change, and the seeking of alternatives. And these ideals carry a special meaning in the ghetto because their attainment is predicated upon separation, isolation, and withdrawal from contact with straight society and induction into the hippie ghetto society. In other words, it is felt that in order to discover and experiment, one must be free of the inhibitions, restraints, and controls upon behavior so necessary to life in the straight society. Thus, the rap session provides the setting in which the ghetto resident learns about his spontaneous desires and urges. He also learns from the behavior of others, notably the elders, as daily experiences and traditional lore are woven together in the ceremonial communication called rapping. Very useful and immediately practical information is thereby passed on as a by-product of the ceremony. Information related to subsistence, approved behavior, gossip, threats and dangers, and alternative ways of living are aired for those who are in need of such information, the initiates into ghetto society.

LSD AND OTHER DRUGS

Before leaving the topic of ritual in ghetto life we must mention briefly why the use of marijuana is in a class apart from other drugs which are used less regularly. For it has been stated that marijuana is *the* drug of choice and the focus of ritualized drug use. This is not to say the use of other drugs is not ritualized. On the contrary, greater ritualization, more esoteric information, and greater secrecy and isolation surround the use of LSD, peyote, methadrine, heroin and other drugs than marijuana. This may seem paradoxical, for the emphasis here has been upon the frequency, universality, and centrality of marijuana use. An inventory of all drugs used in the ghetto is perhaps not necessary in order to have a complete picture. What is necessary is to separate the customs and practices surrounding marijuana use from those which govern the use of other drugs. And for this purpose the drug LSD will be used as an example, mainly because of the tremendous public outcry over its use (for example, see *Newsweek* May 9, 1966:59–64).

A lengthy discussion of the ritual behavior which surrounds LSD, or "acid," is not necessary. It is basically the same as the ritual in which marijuana is the drug of choice, and consists of two parts: the drug ritual and the accompanying ceremonial communication. But the nature of acid as a communal substance is different in many respects from marijuana. First, the supply of LSD is irregular and cannot be as easily procured as marijuana, so that its appearance causes some degree of disruption in the normal social routine. Often this upset causes shifts in quasi-band boundaries and the initiation of new relationships and new patterns of interaction. Second, not all ghetto residents welcome the effects of LSD, and many do not use it. Those who are strong believers in the "quest for self-knowledge" believe in the efficacy of acid for such purposes. But not all residents are enthusiastic enough about this mission to risk a difficult and uncomfortable trip. That is to say, LSD frequently "blows your mind" and gives the individual little control over whether he wishes to be high or higher still. The effects of marijuana can be much more readily controlled by the individual user, who will tailor his use pattern to achieve a desired level of intoxication, altering the amount of smoke inhaled to suit his own tastes. But acid cannot be regulated in this fashion. One usually buys LSD in tablet or capsule form. And a dealer usually will state the supposed amount of the drug contained in the tablet—"ten mikes" or "twenty mikes," meaning ten or twenty micrograms. Yet there is no way to ensure that the dealer's guess is accurate and no way to know whether the LSD is pure or mixed with methadrine. The latter is commonly used to cut LSD while keeping the buyer satisfied, since he will not be aware of the methadrine effects for several hours. In other words, the LSD user generally has no way of knowing the amount of potency of the drug or the nature of the cutting agent contained in any given dosage. At most the user knows his contact or dealer; and dealers make a living on their reputations, so they will seek to maintain good contacts. But not all dealers care about their reputations, and not all users think it important to be aware of the exact contents of the tablets and capsules they "pop," or take orally. Consequently, many residents had had bad trips, in which the desired high was frightening or the dosage too strong or the effects of the cutting agent distasteful. For these reasons—scarcity and lack of confidence in the handling of the drug—LSD did not enjoy widespread popularity.

To questions about the dangers of using the drug and others like it, such as DMT, residents of the ghetto reply that no research has yet proven it harmful.

While this may be true with regard to the physiological effects of the drug (Nowlis 1969:102), it is the psychologicial effects which arouse the great controversy. One LSD user phrased it this way:

> We're fucking with the mind. And that's God, personality, society, and the seat of everything Western society believes in. We're screwing up our adjustment, man; we're messing around with our brains. And brains are holy.

Sociologists Davis and Munoz (1968:157) have noted that hippies profess an "ideologicial mission to turn on the world." The strong feelings of ghetto residents who use LSD are reflected in the comment quoted above. In this light, articles such as "People Using LSD Just 'Playing with Dynamite'" (in the University City newspaper 1966, December 20) are simply viewed as propaganda. And in view of the very impressive array of forces allied against the use of this drug, its popularity can only be accounted for by a very religious kind of sense of mission. Psychologist Keniston (Nowlis, 1969:x) writes of these "apostles of drug use,"

> For them, drug use is a modern-day chemical equivalent to mystical experience, to satori and to the great inward journey of self-exploration and self-discovery.

Or, as one informant reported to the editor of a campus newspaper at State University, "They have the atomic bomb and we have the acid . . . and we hope to win." Apparently the battle lines are drawn and the weapons have been chosen. Along with each newly arrived supply of acid comes the opportunity for a skirmish, the opportunity to pop a pill and separate one's self from the world as it was previously known; to throw caution to the winds; to neglect meals, studies, and daily obligations and routine; to experience visual and auditory and tactile sensations duplicated by no other experience; and to walk among straight people and know that they cannot know what you know, cannot see as you see. Moreover, the drug experience also represents nobility of purpose, the purpose being the possibility of self-discovery. For to be a seeker of visionary experience and mystical insight is to be somehow noble, to have a serious and perhaps holy purpose, and to be above the mundane and routine concern of ordinary men. A "head" is someone who "uses drugs for purposes of mind expansion, insight, and the enhancement of personal attributes, i.e., he uses drugs to discover 'where his head is at'" (Davis and Munoz 1968:160). To be a user of LSD in the hippie ghetto is to be a leader in the "quest for self-knowledge" and to earn the respect of all who agree that to know one's self is one of the highest virtues.

The ideal of self-discovery is given vivid symbolic testimony in the act of taking LSD. For the battleground with those who "have the atomic bomb" is located in each individual, an individual who has been socialized to control emotions, inhibit antisocial behavior, repress urges, and be receptive to the sanctions of group opinion. It is such socialization that must be attacked, broken through, so that an individual is free to discover. It should be emphasized that hippies conceive the experience of taking LSD, as opposed to smoking marijuana, to be an individual act.[1]

---

[1] While the LSD experience is a group activity residents conceive it to be an essentially individual act, or individual experience.

When the observer mentioned to one advocate of such individual voyages of self-discovery that it was hard for him to conceive of learning anything in the absence of the ability to communicate with different people, the comment provoked argument. And in the discussion that followed the observer was accused of being weak, dependent upon others, afraid of himself and his inner feelings, and impotent. In other words, by challenging the notion (not unique to hippies but characteristic also of Western religion) that it was the individual who was the locus of morality, wisdom, insight, and values and by suggesting that these things might be a product of interaction with others in a social situation, the observer challenged the efficacy of the journey of self-discovery. Moreover, he questioned one of the ghetto resident's chief ideologicial supports for the use of LSD—the notion of individualism, individual self-discovery, individual morality, individual responsibility, individual minds, behaviors, and ideals. And there is probably no greater good in the mind of the ghetto resident than the heroic head buffeted by the caprices of ignorant straights but true to his inner, personal values. And we are reminded once again of the heroic Christian of Western mythology journeying to Mount Zion.

But the invectives evoked by the observer's comment point to another strongly held belief: self-discovery is only possible when the individual is vulnerable to that which is to be learned on the inward journey. And vulnerability is perhaps one of the keys to understanding the continued use of LSD. For it is felt that the bad trip results from an inability or unwillingness to confront the confusing, bizarre, and unfamiliar stimuli which reside deep in the subconscious level and are forced up to the level of consciousness by the action of the drug. Earlier it was noted that an unusually potent dosage or a strange cutting agent might have something to do with the bad trip as well. And ghetto residents are aware of this possibility. Still, they explain a bad trip as caused by a fear of vulnerability to unfamiliar stimuli. Thus, some residents are "too uptight" to use the drug. Others do not find vulnerability to be threatening and are felt to be stronger persons. And many informants report bad experiences with the drug, yet they continue to seek its assistance in the quest for self-knowledge. Some residents reported as many as ten consecutive bad trips but still expressed a desire to take LSD again. Apparently it was important for these people to be comfortable with the effects of the drug. Others who experienced consecutive bad trips would frequently stop using the drug for a few months and then try once again to achieve the desired insights and revelations. Others concluded that they were simply not among the elect, that Mount Zion would never be reached.

LSD differs from marijuana in relation to the social organization of the ghetto as well. In the latter part of January, 1968, a supply of acid became available with the arrival of a former ghetto resident from San Francisco. In a very short time the word was circulated that it was "pure stuff, not cut with speed [methadrine]," which indicates to those who use LSD the best possible quality. There was a general air of excitement regarding the newly available supply, and several people purchased some immediately and planned a ritual for that evening. Those who participated in the ritual came from different quasi-bands, but not all the members of each band participated. The excuse offered by the nonparticipants was that studies or work obligations prohibited staying awake all night, for the LSD trip lasts eight to twelve hours on the average. These people were accused by the participants of being "hung up on status" and involved in a world that did not permit self-discovery. This much was obvious from the fact that they were absent. Those who were present had declared themselves ready to embark on the quest. In the ritual which followed, conflict developed as one male-and-female couple engaged in a vicious personal argument before the assembly. They separated early in the evening and each spent the remainder of the trip apart from the other. In the course of the evening the female member of the pair spent most of her time with a single male present, and the male member found himself another female. And soon the two principals who had engaged in the argument were observed to be engaged in love play with their new consorts. Apparently, the argument was not yet over. While this love making did not actually reach the stage of intercourse before the assembly, it was apparent that such was contemplated. One individual in the assembly was upset by this turn of events and chose to leave the room and return to his apartment. He later explained to the observer his reasons: "Those people [the couple who argued and then found new consorts] are really doing bad things to each other, but everything is cool . . . everything is accepted." This individual was shocked, first, by the rapid realignment of mates that occurred and persisted in the following weeks, and, second, by the fact that he had been the only one to leave the room. He concluded, "There's no discrimination. They're like teeny-boppers with drugs, they'll do anything if it gets them off [produces a high]." He felt that the couple involved and the group which approved their behavior by its presence were "copping out" [giving up] and that the couple should have avoided confrontation and conflict before other people and attempted to work out personal problems in private. Perhaps it is gratuitous to add that the other participants that evening felt the behavior of the couple in question and their consorts was acceptable. To the group such a realignment of pair relationships represented an end to the conflict, experimentation with exciting new alternatives, and evidence that those involved were committed to self-discovery and not to archaic norms of behavior. And, one person commented, if it hadn't happened that evening it would have happened another evening.

The situation described above is typical in several ways. First, the introduction of a new exotic drug into the ghetto always produces changes in the social organization. Quasi-bands that normally do not interact find themselves becoming acquainted with each other. Such changes provide the impetus for experimentation in the new atmosphere. Second, the arrival of a new shipment may disturb existing relationships if all concerned do not participate. For example, a male and female living together may both occasionally use the drug but may not be able for various reasons to use it at the same time. Perhaps the male must work that evening or the female has a class she cannot afford to miss, or any number of similar circumstances exist. The arrival of the drug presents the opportunity for dissatisfied couples to end the affair by finding new mates. In fact the couple discussed above probably had decided to separate long before, and the LSD ritual provided the opportunity. Third, perceptual distortions and impaired mental functioning make the atmosphere in which any conflicts or confusions occur a little more cloudy than is normally the case. Possibly, the drug actually contributes to the patterns of shifting relationships and experimentation by making decision making and thinking difficult or inefficient.

But not all LSD rituals involve interpersonal conflict. More often a person finds interpersonal relations tedious. The observer was present upon several occasions when persons would gather for the purpose of tripping. And as often as not the participants spent most of the period in isolation from one another. Many times a person could be observed to be brooding over some problem, idea, or insight, remote and often physically apart from other people. And often a person could be observed to burst out crying or to loose a stream of invectives at himself or another or to laugh to himself. On one such occasion two members of the group assembled for the trip teamed up to help an individual who was feeling particularly miserable. The latter had become deeply morose and complained bitterly about many things. Each time he lapsed into self-pity one of the two helpers would berate him and accuse him of hiding behind his own weakness. As someone later said, "Mike was beautiful. Every time Bill got down and started crying he'd heap shit on his head." And in fact, Mike seemed quite merciless. The other helper, however, played the role of comforter and aid. He gave support through agreement, suggestions, and attempts at distracting his miserable charge's attention, in addition to holding the suffering friend's hand and stroking his palm.

The instance of agonizing suffering cited above and the conflicts cited earlier should serve to underscore the importance of the ideology surrounding LSD in the minds of those who use it. LSD obviously has a significance other than the attainment of kicks or more intense pleasure, for these are not always the result of taking the drug. Often the reverse is true. Yet many continue to take it after several bad experiences. And as one resident said, "We've all seen each other at our worst, when we were just completely broken down and helpless. So we have nothing to hide." Such a self-induced state of vulnerability to painful experiences and pleasurable ones alike, with an attitude of "I'll take whatever I get," cannot be explained simply as a desire for kicks. And it is for this reason that the importance of the belief in individualism, self-discovery, and the quest for self-knowledge has been stressed here.

5 / Values and sentiments

VALUES AND IDEALS

The importance of the "quest for self-knowledge" in the minds of hippie ghetto residents cannot be overemphasized. We have seen that this search provides the ideological support for activities such as the rap session and the use of LSD—activities characteristic of ghetto life and reflective of the ideals of central importance to that life. But simply because ideals are important and are frequently mentioned, we should not conclude they are determinants of behavior. That is to say, the *stated* ideal of the quest for self-knowledge does not explain why ghetto residents behave as they do. This is an important qualification and needs brief elaboration before we proceed further.

As Kluckhohn (1954:388) has stated, "morals—and all group values—are products of social interaction as embodied in culture." It is most accurate, therefore, to speak of valuing rather than values, for we are speaking about a *process* of social life. Values are what we observe people to be doing. Ideals, on the other hand, are the signs and symbols people utilize to explain to themselves (and perhaps to an observer) what they perceive themselves to be doing. Cultural traditions are storehouses of both values and ideals, providing human groups not only with patterns of behavior but also with ready-made explanations that assert the rightness or wrongness of that behavior. Arensberg and Kimball (1965:319) have emphasized the importance of concentrating upon what people actually do day to day, month to month, year to year, in order to understand what they value.

HIPPIES AND VALUES

In Chapter 4 we looked at the ritual rap session in order to determine the more central realities of life in the hippie ghetto. It will be recalled that very little was said of ideology, of spoken beliefs. We did not learn, for example, whether the Vedic scriptures are believed to be very important, what exactly is the nature of beliefs about Christ or Ghandi, what is the significance of Dr. Timothy Leary or Allen Ginsberg in the minds of residents, what is believed about St. Augustine, how hippies relate themselves to the bohemian movements of the past 150 years, and so on. We were concerned with separating values from ideals and with understanding hippie values. This was done by examining interaction in the ritual called the rap session. It was learned that hippies value *isolation* from the larger American society. The decaying mansions of an earlier period in the history of University City provide the hippies with isolation from the bustling, growing duplexes, suburbs, apartment complexes, tract housing projects, and trailer parks which mark the growth of urban America. In the evening the ghetto residents gather to enact the ritual that unites them, to induct neophytes, to make firm once again the vital linkages that weave individuals into groups and groups into networks, and to review once again the stories that compose the legends of past residents or ancestors. It is by keeping these bonds tight and rekindling the memories of the past that the group can exist apart from the larger society, hence, not be dependent upon the institutions of the larger society for subsistence, sex, entertainment, and the other necessities of life. We also learned that hippies value *experimentation* with alternatives to life in the larger society. Sexual unions are not considered binding, friendships must shift with shifting boundaries of quasi-bands, and custom does not regulate behavior as much as the desire to experience something new and exciting. Arrangements concerning housing and sexual relations and subsistence are subjected to the process of experimentation so that communes are spawned, "families" of three persons who share each other's sexual favors exist from time to time, and such jobs as selling drugs on the street or making sandals are innovated. Moreover, by examining the rate of interaction we learned that hippies value *intimacy* in social relations. The rite of intensification occurs almost nightly, and participation is mandatory if one is to be part of the group. It is not uncommon for all members of an associational group to have had sexual relations with several of the other members. The result is that quasi-bands are quite intimate and communication between members of the group takes place in an atmosphere in which there are few secrets, where the persons involved know each other well enough to be able to predict with a high degree of accuracy the behavior of their comrades. The interaction rate among ghetto residents is quite high in certain ritualized situations; and this tells us that they desire and achieve intimate knowledge about their fellows and the world they live in. And the nature of ritualized drug use in the rap session tells us that hippies value *communal intoxication* as a prelude to meaningful verbal communication. Given the fact that the communal drug ritual precedes the act of telling stories, discussing the events of the day, and passing on information, we are left with the conclusion that it is an important ingredient of social discourse. Such ritual intoxication and communication becomes an important boundary marker between quasi-bands, and by it a large body of traditional lore is maintained. Not to participate in the ritual means that one is not really a member of the intimate circle and draws rebuke from those who are participating. Finally, our analysis of the rap session tells us that hippies value *dependency* upon esoteric views of the world. Sources of information outside of the context of ghetto life are considered irrelevant. What is important are the experiences of one's intimate associates. The individual resident, if he is to join the subculture, must study well the networks that lead out of the ghetto to other communities and other opportunities. And, given the fact that drugs which are illegal are kept in circulation through such contacts in the subculture, the high degree of secrecy incumbent upon all members of the network demands of the individual a high degree of commitment to the safety of his fellows. In order to ensure some degree of safety where secrecy is so important, the elders of the quasi-band must be careful that initiates are strongly dependent upon the group. This dependency upon esoteric information is important if males are to escape the draft, for the procedures must be learned from elders. Likewise, information held by the elders regarding subsistence is esoteric and largely passed on in the form of personal recommendation. The neophyte inducted into the group, then, must of necessity be dependent upon a large body of esoteric information.

These then are the values we see reflected in the ritual behavior of residents of the ghetto: isolation and independence from the larger society; experimentation with alternatives to life in the larger society; intimacy in social relations; communal intoxication; and dependency upon esoteric views of the world. To these values we will have to add another that is reflected not in ritual behavior but in the fluctuating levels of interaction intensity and frequency observed during the entire period of study. This sixth value is *transience*, or *mobility*. Opportunities which wax and wane in response to the annual changes in the academic calendar of State University necessarily cause residents of the ghetto to be highly mobile. This is true whether residents are enrolled at State University or whether they market drugs to students, sell the various trappings of the "hippie movement," or earn a living working for one of the many town business concerns which cater to the student population. The hordes of migratory adolescents who are strung out along the highways of America, Europe, and Mexico are in a sense the tangible expression of one of the more important hippie values. To remain free of straight society, to float within the interstices of social life, and to avoid the responsibilities which tie one to a particular location are important if one is to take advantage of fluctuating opportunities. Travel in the network learned in the ghetto is the objective of the entire ghetto life-style, built as it is upon isolation from straights, experimentation, intimacy, communal intoxication, and dependency upon esoteric information. As these values are learned, and the neophytes begin to interact in these ways, they are prepared to leave the ghetto and take advantage of the opportunities which lie beyond the confines of their families, State University, and University City.

IDEALS AND IDEOLOGY

If these values are reflected in social interaction among hippies, what is their relation to hippie ideology? How does the quest for self-knowledge fit with these values? Putting it most succinctly, the quest for self-knowledge, self-discovery, spiritual growth, and the like is part of the cultural tradition of American adolescents. It is an ideal which is part of the cultural universe in which adolescents have been immersed all their lives, and it is to this cultural heritage that hippies turn in an effort to understand and interpret the world in which they find themselves.

The values of isolation, experimentation, intimacy, communal intoxication, dependency upon esoteric information, and transience are expressions of patterns of interaction which have developed among hippies as they have gone about the task of survival—solving the problems of group, sex, subsistence, housing, entertainment, and other conditions of human life. But the explanation, legitimation, and justification of these values consists in an answer to the question, Why? As Wallace (1969) emphasizes, the answer to that question has been drawn from the cultural heritage of Western civilization and Judeo-Christian mythology: the heroic individual pitted against the legions of an evil society and a decadent age, striving for enlightenment, for a blessing, for inclusion among the elect, building the Kingdom of God among the barbarians, disdaining the world of ordinary men in order to achieve the wisdom of the saints. It is particularly significant that it is the individual who must undertake this journey toward self-knowledge and spiritual growth, alone and naked, armed only with an inner strength to persevere. In Western mythology, and especially in America, the individual is the locus of morality, responsibility, attitudes, and values. It is the individual who is immoral, wrong, poorly motivated, sinful, and indolent. It is not the society, community, or social group which fails the individual, but the individual who fails the society, community, or social group. American adolescents who are unhappy, confused, rebellious, or withdrawn quite naturally expect that the problem lies within themselves—within the elusive yet credible "self" which Judeo-Christian mythology explains to be sinful and Western psychology since Freud views as the wellspring of human behavior. It is the "self," then, that must be examined and altered to achieve happiness in Western mythology. Like almost all Westerners, hippies believe they are involved in a process of self-fulfillment and that life is intolerable unless that "self" can be expressed. And like almost all Westerners, they feel that when difficulty is encountered in this process the heroic individual must purge his "self."

Unlike most Westerners, hippies are particularly susceptible to belief in this mythology because at their age and status, they are in a state of limbo. They are in a period of transition called adolescence, a time when they are involved in the culmination of a process of maturation, when choices are to be made that will affect their movement from childhood to adulthood. And it is at this time of vulnerability or susceptibility that some of them have decided to embark on the quest for self-knowledge, deferring for a short time the transition to adulthood and offering the possibility of spiritual growth. In the following chapter we will attempt to answer the questions: Why these people? Why at this time? Why in this place?

6 / The process

The purpose throughout the previous five chapters has been to describe the hippie ghetto from the perspective of the natural history method of community studies. The data were collected and presented in this fashion because of an emphasis, inherent in the method, upon the process of change in an ongoing cultural environment. Now we will turn to a theoretical interpretation of these data, understanding from the beginning that we are dealing with a cultural process and not simply with flat statements about characteristics. In this way it will become apparent how the ghetto is part and product of American society. We will now answer some of the questions posed in earlier chapters.

In no sense can the present effort be said to be a comprehensive treatment of the subject. For example, we have only briefly touched upon the several subcultures fed by the ghetto, concentrating instead upon the neighborhood called the ghetto. Yet this emphasis is significant in that we are concerned with the place of these adolescents in the larger American society and the origin of the groups called subcultures. The assumption has been that there is not a finite number of questions and answers regarding hippies. Rather, we assume that questions have several answers, which may all be valid even if incomplete standing by themselves. For this reason several interpretations of the data are discussed.

ALIENATION AND ANOMIE

It has been stated by many observers that students in American universities are "alienated." The concept of alienation has been greeted in this case study with considered reserve. Alienation, meaning estrangement from society, is useful as a classificatory device, but it is less useful as an analytical device (Clinard 1964:37). The ghosts of Marx and Freud shed such ideological shadows over the concept that one wants to avoid the morass of arguments (witness Melvin Seeman, "On the Meaning of Alienation" in *American Sociological Review, 26,* 1959:784–790). Still, the concept of alienation is useful in signifying that hippies leave the larger society and cease previous patterns of interaction and that they voluntarily choose to drop out of the university. The characteristics of the mental state of alienation as described in a study of university students by a psychologist aid in understanding the depth and totality of this state of separation.

> . . . alienation from American life was almost always a part of a more general alienated ideology, embracing not only attitudes towards the surrounding society, but towards the self, others, groups, and even the structure of the universe and the nature of knowledge (Keniston 1960:56).

This inclusive nature of the mental state of alienation is a feature that will bear more thorough discussion in a moment.

Here it is important to recognize that sociologists have defined situations which tend to produce alienated individuals. Alienation is the manifestation of anomie (normlessness) or the anomic society in terms of the mental state of the individual members of that society (Clinard 1964:37; Merton 1964:226; Misruchi 1964:38). Others have understood anomie to refer to the characteristics of a social system. The character of the anomic social system has received considerable discussion since Merton (1949:281) first formulated the theory after Durkheim's initial coinage of the term in the context of suicide. The theory holds that when a disjunction occurs between cultural goals and institutionalized means for achieving those goals, cultural goals tend to produce deviant behavior (Merton 1949:280–281).

> Anomie refers to a property of a social system, not to the state of mind of this or that individual within the system. It refers to the breakdown of social standards governing behavior and so also signifies little social cohesion. When a high degree of anomie has set in, the rules once governing conduct have lost their savor and their force. Above all else, they are deprived of legitimacy (Merton 1964:226).

The theory of anomie has proven to be an efficient tool in examining the forms of deviance that have traditionally interested sociologists: alcoholism, delinquency, mental disorder, crime, and drug addiction. As such, it may assist in understanding particular forms of deviance associated with hippies. But we must stress that the theory of anomie can carry our analysis only so far. The limits of the usefulness of such typologies are at the point where one must seek their locus in the ongoing processes of social and cultural life. And our objective remains an understanding of the hippie ghetto as part of American culture.

In this regard Merton's (1949:289–308) treatment of individual responses to an anomic social system becomes irrelevant. He lists four types of response—innovation, ritualism, retreatism, and rebellion—all of which may function in the present context as classificatory labels applicable to the hippie ghetto population. Hippies that sell drugs continue to emphasize cultural goals but have innovated illegitimate means by which these goals might be realized. Those who attempt to establish communes and cooperative living arrangements have innovated both goals and means. Those who religiously search for visions and revelations of the true nature of the "self" have responded to anomie by routinizing their lives about a shared cultural goal. Those who turn to alcohol, opium, heroin, morphine, or some other addictive drug have opted for a response Merton would label retreatism. Residents of the ghetto who return to the academic world or enter the business world can be said to be rebels, accepting neither the goals and means of the hippie subcultures nor those of the straight world. Moreover, in reality, all of these responses often find expression in the behavior of a single individual or group.

Clearly the important value of Merton's theory and the labels it provides lies in directing our attention to hippies as examples of alienated individuals and products of an anomic social system. So we must return to an analysis of the social system in which the hippie ghetto operates. Viewed in this manner, responses to alienated mental states and anomic social conditions are seen clearly as products of the social and cultural process in which they occur. That social and cultural process, as has been pointed out earlier, is the rite of passage.

THE RITE OF PASSAGE

Chapple and Coon (1942:484–485) have defined rites of passage after Van Gennep's (1960) initial formulation in 1908. Van Gennep was interested in the way societies provide rituals to govern and control the movement of individuals from one social status to another—rites of initiation, weddings, funerals, and territorial passage. Chapple and Coon (1942:484–485) note that such rites of passage function as mechanisms of transition "to ease the individuals concerned in passing from one state of equilibrium to another." This rite is everywhere divided into three stages: *separation, liminality,* and *incorporation* (Chapple and Coon 1942:484–485; Turner 1969:94). First, the initiate leaves his previous status, ceasing previous patterns of interaction and structured behaviors appropriate to that status. In the present case we have noted that the American adolescent does exactly this as he moves from the confines of his nuclear family of orientation and the high school peer group into a university where he must initiate new and often foreign patterns of interaction. Second, upon separation he begins a period of liminality, or limbo, in which his status is no longer "son of ————" or "daughter of————," but simply student or neophyte. Along with other neophytes of differing talents and backgrounds he learns new behaviors and the traditional knowledge of "elders." He is held in this state of limbo for a specified period during which he experiences various tests and examinations which he must pass before he is allowed to exit. Third, the rite is completed when the individual leaves the educational institution and takes on a new status, different from both previous ones, by which he is incorporated into the larger society as an adult.

The hippie ghetto population, then, consists of liminal persons, or students, who consciously involve themselves in seeking alternatives to the larger society or the status for which they are being prepared by the educational rite. We have seen that they evolve for themselves systems of interaction which make the discovery of alternatives possible. It is apparent, in other words, that hippies have involved themselves in a second rite of passage out of the large institutionalized American rite known as education. This secondary rite, like the primary one, is marked by the three stages of separation, liminality, and incorporation. First, the initiate moves out of participation and interaction in the university, cutting his ties and obligations with professors, parents, and friends. Second, no longer bound by the responsibilities, structured behaviors, and values associated with his previous status, he enters the stage of liminality. During this stage he begins interaction in a new social network, enters a variety of associational groups made up of fellow neophytes and elders of the ghetto. Problems of sex, subsistence, housing, and so forth are now solved in the context of the elder-neophyte relationship. Through this relationship a process of indoctrination occurs in which the neophyte is given the opportunity to adopt values reflected in the behavior of the elders and in the myriad tales and legends conveyed by frequent rituals. The solutions to problems faced by the neophyte involved in the task of living in the ghetto often spark the formation of new associational groups based upon the male-female relationship. Fluctuations in the stability of such relationships over time affect the composition of the ghetto associational groups, and fairly stable networks of interaction gradually emerge. Third, the rite of passage which is ghetto life is completed when the individual is incorporated into one of the several subcultures which represent some feasible adjustment to the larger society.

Rites of passage are always made up of these three parts, but variations may occur depending upon the duration and complexity of interaction (Chapple and Coon 1942:285). In this respect it is interesting to consider Turner's (1968, 1969) extensive treatment of the intervening stage of liminality, because this period and its distinctive symbols have caught the attention of the media and because this stage among American adolescents is often poorly understood by American observers. With regard to the latter point, one sociologist has said:

> Their [adolescents'] presence on the contemporary [hippie] scene is, I think, a function of the institutionalization of adolescence, not simply as the traditional "transitional stage," but as a major period of life. This period may last as long as 20 years, and therefore evokes its own orientational phenomena and behavior . . . (Berger 1967:22).

This prolongation of adolescence is especially true of those who are passing into adulthood through the university system of higher education. The force of the particular orientational phenomena and behaviors of these adolescents was felt rather keenly by the larger society during the 1960s. Still, it should be recognized that adolescents are indeed in a state of limbo; this is a major period of life, to be sure, but it is still a transitional one. The pleas and demands of school administrators, trustees, and state legislatures for "rational action," "responsible dissent," and so on indicate that society continues to view adolescents as dangerous, threatening, and anarchistic (Friedenberg 1966)—traits usually ascribed to those in a state of transition (Turner 1969:109).

The complexities of interaction and duration of the state of liminality which is higher education are probably due to the practical difficulties faced by the adolescent-aged individual in our society. The prominent place of sex and subsistence concerns in the hippie ghetto is probably a function of the prominent place these concerns occupy in adolescence generally. The fact that hippies seek isolation, experimentation, intimacy, communal intoxication, dependency upon esoteric information, and transience in order to solve these problems indicates that few opportunities for solving these problems or, perhaps, even perceiving possible solutions, are offered during their interment in the rite called education. Moreover, adolescents are extremely vulnerable to suggestion, experiments, and change anyway, for the state of liminality is a time of vulnerability to new ideas and new behaviors.

The individual is free of constraints and controls upon behavior, since he lacks a definite status. The armed forces take advantage of the effects of liminality to train and discipline recruits and draftees; a college fraternity processes its initiates in the same fashion; and the system of higher education is no different. Liminality is a process so universal that its workings may not be well understood, and it is important enough in the present context to be discussed at length.

Liminal periods are characterized everywhere by "structural impoverishment and symbolic enrichment" (Turner 1968:576). The previous symbols of status, identifying a person as occupying a position in a stable social system, are cast off. Hippie ghetto residents replace such symbols with insignia that are wholly unintelligible to their former associates and straight society as a whole, symbols that are translated as "weird," "bizarre," or even "crazy" by those who obtain no enjoyment from the unusual. Shoulder-length hair on males; hemlines that fall to about the pubic region of females; conglomerate, gaudy jewelry for both sexes; and esoteric signs and sayings are examples of symbols that may have meaning only to those who are similarly separated from the status system of the larger society. What is more, symbols which carry very definite meaning in straight society— for example, uniforms and military insignia and American flags—are adopted in a new context where they carry esoteric meaning. Symbolic enrichment among hippies is so obvious, being the main point of fascination to the media, that it needs little demonstration here.

More significant, perhaps, than shoulder-length hair on males is the absence of structured, differentiated, hierarchical behavior and the presence of "undifferentiated *comitatus*" (Turner 1969:96). The Latin word *comitatus* refers to a feeling of fellowship, but the writer prefers the related Latin word *comitas*, meaning politeness, civility, and kindness. We have seen this reflected in the drug rites, in the way in which shifts in group membership occur, and in the belief that residents of the ghetto are involved in a process of self-discovery or spiritual growth. In the hippie ghetto life is to be lived "now." Spontaneity is a vehicle for self-discovery. Experimentation is highly valued, and all manner of behavior is considered "beautiful" if it is recognized as an expression of the "self." Even hostile and aggressive acts are received in the spirit of *comitas*, for they teach an individual about himself and others; such acts are not only welcomed but encouraged, since they are evidence of trust in one's fellows and commitment to the quest for self-knowledge. Liminality is a "moment in and out of time" where none of the temporal responsibilities, inhibitions, and rules apply (Turner 1969:96).

Liminality is "essentially a period of returning to first principles and taking of the cultural inventory" (Turner 1968:577). Spontaneity and experimentation deliver a host of stimuli heretofore sublimated by the demands of a previous status and structure, for to be without a social position is to be in a state of limbo and to cease to have a specific perspective.

> [It is] in a sense to become (at least potentially) aware of all positions and arrangements and to have a total perspective. What converts potential understanding into real gnosis is instruction (Turner 1968:577).

And so the kaleidoscope of stimuli is transmuted into knowledge and is imbued with meaning through communication with elders. Urges, fantasies, and fears press for recognition and attention. These may directly produce insights and thus are encouraged and even directly produced by ceremonial sacraments and ceremonial behaviors.

Liminality is a time of freedom when the normal moral codes have little validity and are transgressed (Turner 1968:577). Sexual relations are not binding, for example. Responsibilities are minimal. Interaction tends to fluctuate with opportunity, mood, and temperament rather than with custom. Experimentation in courtship produces exotic arrangements of males and females, and transgression of existing male-female relational boundaries occurs among the individual's most intimate associates and friends. The individual who leaves the associational group is the one who seeks to cement relations and declare his mate "ineligible" to potential rivals. Those who transcend the moral codes of straights remain secure in liminal freedom and actively participate in experimentation. And it will be remembered that to residents of the ghetto a bad trip on LSD symbolizes an inability to give in freely to the effects of the drug, a failure to submit to vulnerability to new stimuli, and a negative reliance upon traditional mechanisms of control in an effort to avoid unwelcome effects.

In the nightly rites of intensification one finds natural expressions of liminal symbols, for such expression is the nature of ritual. The feelings of camaraderie and companionship are induced by ritual acts such as sharing the sacramental drug and voicing expressions of satisfaction and contentment and by ritual beliefs such as the expectation that the sacrament will produce a shared psychic state in which all the participants are drawn together. Ordinary communication is held in abeyance while ceremonial communication symbolizes "honesty," a truer expression of the self, or, in Turner's (1969:103) more lyrical words, "whole men in relation to other whole men." The participants move like holy men in a temple, passing the pipe about the room in the expectation of a desired state of rapport. And it is in the nightly rites of intensification that the mythology of the quasi-band is aired. Functioning as an integral part of the indoctrination of initiates, such tales demonstrate how the world is to be viewed, what values are important, and what is expected of members of the group. Also, they provide information that will be useful to the neophyte at a later time, as he leaves the ghetto.

To Turner (1968) the major importance of these myths, however, lies in their ontological value. For the liminal wisdom of the elders is passed on and "refashions the very being of the neophyte," infusing him with power (Turner 1969:103).

[Myths] are felt to be high or deep mysteries which put the initiant temporarily into close rapport with the primary or primordial generative powers of the cosmos, the acts which transcend rather than transgress the norms of human secular society (Turner 1968:577).

The neophyte, stripped of defenses and vulnerable, floating in the limbo of transition, and freed of any secure structural relations and responsibilities, is thereby given power in the form of esoteric knowledge to confront the forces of the world. Cloaked in unresponsibility, innocent of guilt or shame, invulnerable to the threats that stem from transition and change, he is prepared to leave the ghetto.

What the initiant seeks through rite and myth is not a moral exemplum so much as the power to transcend the limits of his previous [state] (Turner 1968:577).

A large old home reminiscent of a once more prosperous era is being prepared for the opening of a Free School. The school is planned by one quasi-band which hopes to offer eventually a range of courses to students of all ages taught by individuals who donate their time and skill. (Photo by author)

Hippie ghetto life, then, may be interpreted as a rite of passage out of the role and status of a university student and into membership in a subculture. The separation of the initiate from higher education is seen to be quite effective. Likewise, the liminal state operates as an effective device through which the initiate is socialized and tested and given the power to make this transition. But the hippie rite of passage is less effective as a mechanism of incorporation into an alternate state of equilibrium. This is evident from two facts mentioned earlier: first, a plurality of subcultural groups are the end product of the process; second, transience and mobility are two important values communicated to the neophyte. Both of these facts mean that full-time commitment to a subcultural group is not expected to be common. A certain amount of uneasiness with completing the rite of passage might be expected; and in fact many find leaving University City rather traumatic, recognizing that traveling the networks of a subcultural group is as much a matter of good fortune as it is skill. Thus the possibility of returning to a period of liminality and striking out in another direction always exists for the individual who is dissatisfied. And some individuals are perpetually dissatisfied, perpetually afraid to leave. But much of this must be inferred and perhaps does not warrant discussion, since our topic has not been the subcultural groups, but the generative process of many different groups, of life in the ghetto.

Returning to the discussion of alienation and anomie at the beginning of this chapter, it can now be seen why such labels and the taxonomic responses they project could tell us very little of the kind of deviant called hippie. And this is true if only because hippies bear many similarities to university students; in fact, many are students. Even the casual reader could not fail to see that many of the behaviors and values and symbols described in previous chapters as typical of residents of the ghetto in the late 1960s are quite common on university campuses in general. Does this mean that most students are alienated? Does it mean that American society is becoming more anomic? Are all students deviates? Or does it mean that what was called the "hippie movement" in the late 1960s is alive and growing? The answers to these questions can probably best be discovered by looking at the nature of such movements.

7 / The hippie movement

THE REVITALIZATION PROCESS

Margaret Mead (1947:645) discussed the implications of culture change for personality development among the very people about whom this essay is written, noting:

> The capacity to organize experience in terms of a cultural reality inherent in growing up in a homogeneous culture is lost among the children of those who have themselves undergone the first impact of change. As a result perceived experience becomes atomized into units which have no structural relationship to a whole that can no longer be perceived (1947:644).

She predicted then, twenty-four years ago, the appearance of movements which would turn to "inner rhythms." Many contemporary writers have expressed this opinion. Yet the hippie ghetto has been described here not as the spawning ground of a social movement, but as a rite of passage. This may seem curious to those already familiar with Wallace's (1956) treatment of the procedural stages of the revitalization movement. When one considers the definition of such a movement it becomes apparent that those who live in the hippie ghetto are moving in the direction of, if they do not already represent, the revitalization process. A revitalization movement is defined as:

> "a deliberate, organized, conscious effort by members of a society to construct a more satisfying culture" (Wallace 1956:265).

It is apparent that those who seek out and find alternative ways of living in an effort to reshape their lives into something more gratifying and fulfilling than before are engaging themselves in a revitalization effort.

Rather than choose at this point between two theoretical interpretations—that of the rite of passage and that of a revitalization effort—we should look at the structural similarities between the two processes. Both Turner (1969:111–112) in his discussion of "ritual process," of which rites of passage are the most notable, and Wallace (1956:271) in his discussion of the revitalization process have remarked on the intriguing structural similarities between the two processes.

Revitalization movements have long held the attention of American anthropologists. Some of the most well-known and most thoroughly studied of these are the Christian movement, Mohammedanism, the Ghost Dance religion, the New Religion of Handsome Lake, Cargo cults, and the Protestant Reformation. We will return to a discussion of these examples in a moment. For now it is important to note that movements that we call revitalistic are religious movements which arise out of situations of extreme individual and societal stress and extreme distortion of a cultural gestalt. These movements arise at times when it becomes increasingly difficult for individual members of a society to follow culturally patterned ideals, behaviors, and beliefs—at times of deprivation and pain, starvation, disease, depopulation, warfare, uncontrollable innovation, factionalism, and other natural catastrophes which spell change for the culture and its bearers. It is in such periods of change and crisis that revitalization movements appear to be born. Obviously, some movements for political independence (for example, Black Muslims), nationalistic movements (for example, Communist revolution in China), and colonial rebellions (for example, Mau Mau movement) have religious aspects and frequently may be interpreted as revitalization efforts. We say that these examples and others which may appear even more disparate are revitalistic because they manifest the processural structure of a revitalization movement.

The subject of revitalization movements and cultural change is too broad, too complex, to be given lengthy discussion here. The interested reader is referred to Wallace's *Religion: An Anthropological View* (1966) for further clarification of some of the points introduced below. Our purpose is simply to explore the relationship between rites of passage and revitalization movements as it is reflected in the "hippie movement."

The period of individual stress which is the beginning stage of the revitalization process is characterized by attempts on the part of various members of a society to ameliorate the effects of stress and distortion. Perhaps one individual, perhaps several here and there, experiment with various innovative techniques for reducing the effects of a new high level of stress, whatever it might be in a given instance. These individuals are frequently marginal members of society, less subject to the traditional sanctions and controls applied to individual members of that society. They are frequently able to experiment when other persons with more secure and definite social status are less able to innovate due to the obligations and responsibilities incumbent upon them by virtue of that definite social status. The effort to reduce high levels of stress is what Wallace calls "mazeway reformulation":

> The mazeway is nature, society, culture, personality, and body image, as seen by one person. . . . Changing the mazeway involves changing the total *Gestalt* of his image of self, society, and culture, of nature and body, and of ways of action (1956:266–267).

Stress and distortion are extremely important in this context for they imply that traditional stress-reducing techniques are worthless and no longer reduce stress. For example, the stress-reducing technique might be eating, praying, or sexual intercourse in society Z. Certain changes in the ecological and sociological circumstances of the society may reduce the effectiveness of, say, eating as a stress-reducing technique. Famine or warfare or conquest may make the traditional beliefs and behaviors which surround this technique meaningless in the new, changed cultural circumstances. When this occurs the result is far-reaching: "admission that a major [stress-reducing] technique is worthless is extremely threatening because it implies that the whole mazeway system may be inadequate" (Wallace 1956:269). Individuals, then, who recognize the ineffectiveness of major stress-reducing techniques strive to innovate others which will produce the desired effect. And this necessarily leads to a second stage in the revitalization process.

This stage is called "cultural distortion," and it occurs after several individuals have attempted various innovations. It occurs because by making certain fundamental changes in their lives these individuals have made fundamental changes in the cultural gestalt, or the organization of and relationships between elements in the cultural universe. Thus, in the hypothetical example used above, members of society Z who felt eating to be an ineffective stress-reducing technique might have innovated fasting, prayer, and rigorous exercise as devices which worked to reduce stress for them. Such innovations would affect the nature of their beliefs and attitudes towards traditional notions of what was "proper" food, what was the "proper" way food was to be prepared and consumed, and which of the important figures in the cultural mythology were to be propitiated through prayer. Such individuals might seize upon completely obscure foods, behaviors, and deities in the cultural tradition and elevate them to a new level of importance which would appear unique and strange in the eyes of their fellows. Or they might seize upon elements that were foreign or part of another cultural tradition altogether, which in the eyes of their fellows might make the innovators appear not just a little strange but perhaps insane. In any case, the innovation and experimentation with new elements, foods, behaviors, beliefs, and attitudes would demand a reorganization of the cultural gestalt downgrading certain accepted elements and elevating less popular elements. The result would be as follows:

> Rigid persons apparently prefer to tolerate high levels of chronic stress rather than make systematic adaptive changes in the mazeway. More flexible persons try out various limited mazeway changes in their personal lives, attempting to reduce stress by addition or substitution of mazeway elements with more or less concern for the *Gestalt* of the system (Wallace 1956:269).

Society then begins to fractionate as experimentation, addition, and substitution of elements occupy some of its members and not others. Such innovation will be more or less successful, and stress may or may not be reduced among the innovators. But in any event the cultural gestalt is distorted by such changes.

Now the stage of revitalization actually begins with what Wallace (1956:270) calls "mazeway reformulation." He notes that in all cases with which anthropologists are familiar mazeway reformulation occurs "as a moment of insight" to a prophet or "one of several hallucinatory visions by a single individual" in which the supernatural explains current difficulties, troubles, and stresses as resulting from the violation of certain dogmas. The prophet then reveals his insights as doctrine to potential converts and organizes his followers. The doctrine is adapted to the resistance such movements inevitably meet, transforms the culture, and is finally routinized (Wallace 1956:273–274). The examples that support this generalization are legion: Christ and Christianity, Mohammed in the Near East, Jomo Kenyatta in Kenya, Wovoka of the Ghost Dance religion, John Slokum of the Shakers, John Wesley's Methodism, and Dekanawidah of the Handsome Lake religion—to give a few.

THE "HIPPIE MOVEMENT"

Returning to the hippie movement, we can now ask what similarities and what differences obtain between it and the processural structure sketched above. In short, is the so-called "hippie movement" properly interpreted as a contemporary revitalization movement in American culture? Of particular interest are some striking similarities between Wallace's (1956:266–277) conception of mazeway reformulation and Keniston's (1960:56) characterization of the mental state of alienated students. Each involves changes in the total cultural gestalt; the nature of society, self, culture, personality; the nature of the body; the structure of the universe; and the nature of knowledge. Each involves changes in the ways in which these things are perceived and the ways in which they are related to each other. Likewise, Turner (1969:121) has called attention to the "peculiar linkages between personality, universal values, and 'spirit' or 'soul' that appear to be the stigmata of communitas." These investigators, then, have found some characteristics to be typical both of individuals involved in mazeway reformulation and individuals occupying a state of liminality in a rite of passage. In each process basic alterations of the cultural gestalt occur, probably because in each process new elements of the cultural universe are explored, experimented with, and adopted. And this necessarily means reorganization of the former gestalt.

Another striking similarity in the structures of the two processes is the importance of ritualization of interaction or ceremonial behavior. Wallace (1956) in his earlier writings places emphasis upon the importance of the evolution of a dogma or belief in a set of rules; but in more recent writings, he stresses the relatively greater importance of the rituals in which such beliefs are expressed. Wallace (1966:199) points out that:

> . . . it is ritual, and not myth, which does the actual work of conflict resolution, and perhaps the most dramatic examples of both the ritual resolution of discontinuities and of contradictions [in the cultural gestalt] are provided by the widespread customs of puberty rituals and other rites of passage.

We have seen in previous chapters the importance of ritualized interaction in the lives of hippies. Similarly, in the revitalization movement ritual functions to reduce conflict and stress, to draw its participants together, and to affirm the belief of its practitioners in certain myths. Be it a communion sacrament, an exhausting round of dancing and singing, a rigorous series of body movements accompanying prayerful thoughts, or the monotonous repetition of certain vocables in time with a water drum, the ritual is the central activity of those involved in the revitalization movement, for only through its enactment are their desires fulfilled and the ends of certain stated beliefs served. Only through enactment of the ritual is revitalization achieved, converts inducted, and the already faithful made secure and content in their belief.

It is true, then, that the rite of passage of life in the ghetto and certain characteristics of the processural structure of a revitalization movement bear marked similarities. There is, however, greater dissimilarity. For example, the previous pages give little evidence of prophets as such in the hippie ghetto. Although one could conceive of such a figure as the "original dropout," he is not generally well known in the ghetto. Some observers have posited relationships between hippies and various bohemian movements, but it is difficult to see any real connection, especially given the proliferation of various hippie cults devoted to nudity, vegetables, drugs, Jesus, Krishna, rock music, sexual sensuality, and so on. And prophetic figures such as Allen Ginsberg, Dr. Timothy Leary, Picasso, or Gertrude Stein are simply not that important in the lives of the ghetto informants. Certainly these figures' "teachings" are not considered doctrine or dogma, and to the observer's knowledge no one has come forth to claim credit for inventing the rap session. What is certain is that ritual behaviors and beliefs engage the neophyte in what he perceives as a quest for self-knowledge, or personal vision seeking, but no single vision points the way to doctrine and no single person is treated with special respect in this regard. There are only elders in the ghetto, who by virtue of longevity command a great knowledge of the mythology of a certain quasi-band and who are known to have previously confronted many problems which may appear new and frightening to the neophyte. Elders, then, may act as guides or models, but their teaching and direction do not involve well-defined practices and programs through which the good life is to be achieved. Moreover, the paths out of the ghetto are numerous and most are forked; so in this sense each individual must choose his own alternatives according to the promptings of his self and the knowledge gained from the elders.

It might appear, then, that even though students and former students in the ghetto seem to be engaged in a process of creating alternatives and seeking a more satisfying way of life, we could not characterize that effort as revitalistic in the absence of some prophetic figure. If that were the case—and it probably is not—we might view the social process of ghetto life as a form of "milieu therapy," much the same as Werner (1963:259–267) has in the case of student religious centers on a university campus. One might reach this conclusion if residents returned to the university or in some other way joined the larger society after a therapeutic sojourn in the ghetto, but many in fact do find alternatives to the larger society. Various networks lead to communes, drug marketing, drug addiction, and such, which are variously successful and viable alternatives, but alternatives nonetheless. Some degree of mazeway reformulation is indicated when a young man born and raised in a middle-class suburb decides to grow vegetables in Canada or an adolescent girl from a similar sociocultural background decides to sell heroin on the streets of New York. A closer look at the role of the prophet in revitalization movements seems to be called for.

It seems that there is reason to question the emphasis upon the role of the prophet and hallucinatory visions experienced by a single individual. Antonio Counselheiro [Anthony the counselor], an individual to whom later generations attributed the role of prophet in the Brazilian backlands during the nineteenth century, was a weak and pathetic figure who sought solitude in the wilderness, not followers or disciples. His role appears to have been shaped by the actions of the *sertanejos*, or backlanders, whose frustrations, anxieties, deprivations, beliefs, and desires found expression in the figure of Counselheiro. Reading Da Cunha (1945) one cannot escape the conclusion that the prophet was a vehicle not for the supernatural but for the reformulation and assertion of *sertanejo* cultural beliefs and ideology. Likewise, Wovoka, the Paiute prophet of the Ghost Dance religion during the late nineteenth century on the North American Plains, never proselytized his millennial vision. His followers journeyed to the Paiute reservation and sought him out. For it was the visionary, mystical beliefs typical of the northern tribes which were asserted. As Mooney (1965) emphasizes, the noble Sioux, Cheyenne, and Arapaho needed no prophet to convince them to look to the future for cataclysmic salvation from their inhuman bondage on the reservations. Along these lines Nash (1955) has argued that the deprivation and hardship suffered by the Klamath, Modoc, and Paviotso peoples explain their ready acceptance of not one but several different prophets and three different revitalization efforts: the Ghost Dance, the Earthlodge cult, and later the Dreaming. Clearly, the prophet could not have been crucially important, for these peoples accepted several. Similarly, Worsley (1968) has emphasized much the same interpretation in Melanesia, where prophets arise in quick succession with varying doctrines and millennial predictions only to disappear in a short time. Prophets come and go, but the conditions which produce Cargo cults, as Melanesian revitalization movements are called, are apparently constant.

As Worsley (1968:xiv) points out in his new introduction to *The Trumpet Shall Sound*, a prophet can die, be imprisoned, or simply relinquish the role of leader and still the movement continues. Traits of personal charisma, skills of leadership, or force of personality are apparently not the critical ingredients. What is needed, perhaps, are conditions of deprivation and hardship, a doctrine or message formulated out of the cultural traditions, and a ritual for reducing high levels of stress and reinforcing belief in the doctrine. The seeds of such movements do not have to be contained in the visions of a Wovoka or a Counselheiro, but in the traditions stretching forward and backward in time in which people have been taught to believe by parents and grandparents and which they will transmit to their children. The conditions of hardship and deprivation prepare the ground and make it fertile and receptive to such formulations and reformulations of a cultural tradition.

In the present case, hippies have reformulated the Judeo-Christian tradition of individual salvation, individual guilt and sin, the journey of spiritual growth, and created an ideology we have seen to be the "quest for self-knowledge." As Malinowski has pointed out, mythology functions as a warrant, a charter, and sometimes as a practical guide to activity; it is believed to be the "real cause which has brought about the moral rule, the social grouping, the rite, or the custom" (Malinowski 1954:108). As we saw in Chapter 5 on values and sentiments, it is the role of ideas such as the quest for self-knowledge to explain, justify, and give legitimacy to values which are reflected in social interaction. Ideas, myths, and ideologies are easily molded. The test of their validity lies in their applicability to human interaction.

Social anthropologists have long defined social groups in terms of such collective symbolic action (Chapple and Coon 1942:507; Malinowski 1954:108; Warner 1959:450). The central realities of the lives of any group of people will be emphasized and reflected in such symbolic expressions as ritual and ceremony. And it is ritual activity which concerns us most, for it can be safely maintained that most Americans subscribe to the validity of many of the points of the hippie ideology. Most Americans believe in the Judeo-Christian notions of individual salvation through good works; spiritual growth through communion and meditation and prayer; and individual guilt and sin. But there are many kinds of Americans, and Judeo-Christian mythology receives symbolic expression in the rites of literally hundreds of differing sects. The divisions among these sects are based not on minute doctrinal differences but on the interpretation of these differences and their expression in human interaction, ritual affirmation of membership, ritual rededication to the differences which symbolize the distinction between "us" and the "outsiders," and ritual expression of the rightness of a particular interpretation of an almost two-thousand-year-old tradition. Hippies are not any different in this regard. They exist and are defined as a group because they have created a ritual and environment which defines them so. Any assemblage of people is not a group. A group must conceive itself as a unit, and it does this by ritual activity in which its reasons for existence are symbolically held up for all to see.

What does this tell us of the "hippie movement?" It tells us that it matters little if the hippie ideology has been picked up by more and more students. Likewise, the lengths of students' hair, the clothes they wear, the symbols they stick on their car windows, and so on are more the work of Madison Avenue advertisers who make it their business to seek out points of vulnerability than increasing evidence of the spread of a movement. Students occupy a liminal status and are thus vulnerable to the same kinds of stresses and pressures hippies experience. Students are very receptive while they hang there in limbo (Kimball 1962, Spindler 1972).

One can only speak of the spread of the "hippie movement" when the mechanism by which it is maintained is spreading: ritual drug use and communication. The movement consists of a set of values and a pattern of human interaction that are maintained by those who participate in the rite of intensification. The movement can grow only as the rite of intensification becomes more popular, for it is this rite which makes possible the perpetuation of the values of isolation, experimentation, intimacy, communal intoxication, dependency upon esoteric information, and transience. These values will become important to other students besides hippies if the stresses and cultural distortions which stem from transition to adulthood in American society become increasingly intolerable.

References

American Medical Association, 1966, "Editorial." *Journal of the American Medical Association, 198:*658.

Arensberg, Conrad M., and Solon T. Kimball, 1965, *Culture and community.* New York: Harcourt Brace Jovanovich, Inc.

Barnett, Homer G., 1957, *Indian shakers.* Carbondale, Ill.: Southern Illinois University Press.

Becker, Howard S., 1963, *Outsiders: studies in the sociology of deviance.* New York: The Free Press.

Berger, Bennett M., 1967, "Hippie morality: More old than new." *Trans-action, 5:* 19–23.

Brown, Joe David, ed., 1967, *The hippies.* New York: Time, Inc., Book Division.

Chapple, Eliot D., and Carleton S. Coon, 1942, *Principles of anthropology.* New York: Holt, Rinehart and Winston, Inc.

Clinard, Marshall B., 1964, *Anomie and deviant behavior.* New York: The Free Press.

Da Cunha, Euclides, 1945, *Rebellion in the backlands.* Chicago: University of Chicago Press.

Davis, Fred, 1967, "Why all of us may be hippies some day." *Trans-action, 5:* 10–18.

Davis, Fred, and Laura Munoz, 1968, "Patterns and meaning of drug use among hippies." *Journal of Health and Social Behavior, 9:* 156–164.

Feldman, Harvey, 1968, "Ideological supports to becoming and remaining a heroin addict." *Journal of Health and Social Behavior, 9:* 131–139.

Foulks, Edward F., and Russel Eisenman, 1969, "An analysis of a peer network using psychedelic drugs." *Psychiatric Quarterly, 43* (3): 389–395.

Friedenberg, Edgar, 1966, "Adolescence as a social problem." In *Social problems: a modern approach.* Howard S. Becker, ed. New York: John Wiley and Sons, Inc.

Goffman, Irving, 1961, *Asylums.* New York: Doubleday & Company, Inc.

Henry, Jules, 1965, *Culture against man.* New York: Random House, Inc.

Hollister, Leo E., 1971, "Marihuana in man: three years later." *Science, 172:* 21–29.

Keniston, Kenneth, 1960, *The uncommitted: alienated youth in American society.* New York: Harcourt Brace Jovanovich, Inc.

Kimball, Solon T., 1962, "Social science research and higher education." *Human Organization 21* (4): 271–279.

———, 1966, "Individualism and the formation of values." *Journal of Applied Behavioral Science, 2* (4): 465–482.

Kimball, Solon T., and James E. McClellan, Jr., 1966, *Education and the new America.* New York: Random House, Inc.

Klein, Julius, and Derek L. Phillips, 1968, "From hard to soft drugs: temporal and substantive changes in drug usage among gangs in a working-class community." *Journal of Health and Social Behavior, 9:* 139–145.

Kluckhohn, Clyde, 1954, "Values and value orientation in the theory of action." In *Toward a general theory of action*. Talcott Parsons and Edward Shils, eds. Cambridge, Mass.: Harvard University Press.

Linton, Ralph, 1936, *The study of man*. New York: Appleton-Century-Crofts.

Malinowski, Bronislaw, 1964, *Magic, science, and religion and other essays*. New York: Doubleday & Company, Inc.

Mead, Margaret, 1947, "The implications of culture change for personality development." *American Journal of Orthopsychiatry, 17:* 633–646.

Merton, Robert K., 1949, "Social structure and anomie: revisions and extensions." In *The family: its function and destiny*. Ruth Ansberg, ed. New York: Harper & Row, Publishers.

———, 1964, "Anomie, anomia, and social interaction." In *Anomie and deviant behavior*. Marshall B. Clinard, ed. New York: The Free Press.

Misruchi, Ephraim H., 1964, *Success and opportunity: a study of anomie*. New York: The Free Press.

Mooney, James, 1965, *The ghost dance religion*. Chicago: University of Chicago Press.

Nash, Phillio, 1955, "The place of religious revivalism in the formation of the intercultural community on Klamath Reservation." In *Social anthropology of North American Indian tribes*. Fred Eggan, ed. Chicago: University of Chicago Press. Pp. 377–442.

Nowlis, Helen H., 1969, *Drugs on the college campus*. New York: Doubleday & Company, Inc.

Polsky, Ned, 1967, *Hustlers, beats, and others*. Chicago: Aldine Publishing Company.

Seeman, Melvin, 1959, "On the Meaning of Alienation." *American Sociological Review, 26:* 784–790.

Service, Elman R., 1962, *Primitive social organization*. New York: Random House, Inc.

Solomon, David, 1966, *The marijuana papers*. New York: New American Library of World Literature, Inc.

Spindler, George D., 1973, "The education of adolescents: an anthropological perspective." In *Education and cultural process*. George D. Spindler, ed. New York: Holt, Rinehart and Winston, Inc.

Spindler, George D., and Louise Spindler, 1971, *Dreamers without power: the Menomini Indians*. New York: Holt, Rinehart and Winston, Inc.

Subcommittee on Alcoholism and Narcotics, 1971, "Marijuana and health: a report to the Congress from the Secretary, Department of Health, Education, and Welfare." Washington, D.C.: Government Printing Office.

Turnbull, Colin M., 1961, *The forest people*. New York: Simon and Schuster, Inc.

Turner, Victor W., 1968, "Myth and symbol." In *International Encyclopedia of the Social Sciences*. New York: Crowell-Collier-Macmillan, Inc., and The Free Press. *10:* 576–581.

———, 1969, *The ritual process: structure and anti-structure*. Chicago: Aldine Publishing Company.

Van Gennep, Arnold, 1960, *The rites of passage*. Chicago: University of Chicago Press.

Wallace, Anthony F. C., 1956, "Revitalization movements." *American Anthropologist, 58:* 264–281.

———, 1959, "Cultural determinants of response to hallucinatory experience." *American Medical Association Archives of General Psychiatry, 1:* 58–69.

———, 1966, *Religion: an anthropological view*. New York: Random House, Inc.

———, 1969, "The trip." In *Psychedelic drugs: proceedings of a Hahnemann Medical College and Hospital symposium by the Department of Psychiatry.*

Richard E. Hicks and Paul J. Fink, eds. New York: Grune & Stratton, Inc. Pp. 151–156.

Warner, W. Lloyd, 1959, *Living and the dead: a study of the symbolic life of Americans*. New Haven, Conn.: Yale University Press.

Weil, Andrew T., Norman E. Zinberg, and Judith M. Nelsen, 1968, "Clinical and psychological effects of marijuana in man." *Science, 162:* 1234–1242.

Werner, Fred, 1963, "Acculturation and milieu therapy in student transition." In *Education and culture*. George D. Spindler, ed. New York: Holt, Rinehart and Winston, Inc.

Winick, Charles, 1959–1960, "The use of drugs by jazz musicians." *Social Problems, 7:* 240–253.

Worsley, Peter, 1968, *The trumpet shall sound*. Rev. ed. New York: Schocken Books.

Recommended Reading

Conrad M. Arensberg and Solon T. Kimball. *Culture and Community.* New York: Harcourt Brace Jovanovich, 1965.

For the student who wishes to study further the natural history method in social anthropology, particularly in regard to studies of American cultures, Drs. Arensberg and Kimball provide the clearest discussion of the theoretical model and empirical techniques together with illustrative ethnographic data drawn from their own fieldwork in North America and Northern Europe.

Howard S. Becker. *Outsiders: Studies in the Sociology of Deviance.* New York: The Free Press, 1963.

Becker's work is unique in several ways to the usual sociological studies of deviance, for he emphasizes the significance of social context and social setting in understanding human behavior, while he simultaneously collects data through the technique of participant observation rather than the standard sociologicial questionnaire.

Joe David Brown. *The Hippies.* New York: Time, Inc., Book Division, 1967.

A collection of essays by *Time* writers, this book is valuable as a chronicle of the years 1966 and 1967 when the mass media discovered the hippie movement. At the very least, the reader will gain an understanding of the tenor of the public reaction to the phenomenon.

Solon T. Kimball, and James E. McClellan, Jr. *Education and the New America.* New York: Random House, Inc., 1966.

In this perplexing and intriguing volume, the authors dissect the underpinnings of the traditional education system in America and argue that change is essential, given the dramatic changes (and well-documented here) in the nature of American society. A basic work for any student interested in modern American culture or the emerging role of education in that culture.

Theodore Roszak. *The Making of a Counter Culture: Reflections on the Technocratic Society and Its Youthful Opposition.* New York: Doubleday & Company, Inc., 1969.

Theodore Roszak's treatment of "technocracy's children" is one of the best of its kind. The author feels strongly that the problems of contemporary America can be solved by a carefully constructed conglomeration of the ideological positions of hippies, radicals, black separatists, Marxism, Zen Buddhism, liberated women, and the New Left. What he sees emerging from this marriage is called the counter culture. The book's major weakness is the absence of any discussion of empirical evidence and its concentration upon the spoken and written word. The result is a stimulating if ethereal discussion of many of the major issues of the 1960s together with an excellent bibliography of commentators on these and other issues bearing on the subject of youth.

George D. Spindler. "The Education of Adolescents: An Anthropological Perspective." In *Education and Cultural Process,* edited by George D. Spindler. New York: Holt, Rinehart and Winston, Inc., 1973.

Utilizing the comparative data available to the anthropologist, Spindler interprets the place of education cross-culturally and relates the findings to problems of education in contemporary America. In this fashion be is able to explain many behaviors of American students that have confounded others.

Victor W. Turner. *The Ritual Process: Structure and Anti-structure.* Chicago: Aldine Publishing Company, 1969.

Perhaps the most thorough treatment of the rites of passage since Van Gennep's cross-cultural survey of these rituals is in this text. Working from his own field research in Africa, Turner successfully integrates his findings into an analysis of the writings of Buber and others who have sought to define the institutional place of *communitas;* and in so doing he presents a striking example of the relevance of anthropological research and data in understanding contemporary issues.

Arnold Van Gennep. *The Rites of Passage.* Chicago: University of Chicago Press, 1960.

Van Gennep's work is a classic in the field of anthropology, dealing with rites involving a transition or change in status on a worldwide basis. An introduction by Solon T. Kimball gives evidence of the contemporary significance of Van Gennep's studies and questions why his work has been largely ignored by the sister social sciences of anthropology that necessarily deal with aspects of change.

Anthony F. C. Wallace. *Religion: An Anthropological View.* New York: Random House, Inc., 1966.

In an effort to analyze religious behavior on a cross-cultural basis, Wallace discusses religious phenomena ranging from Jung's psychoanalytical theories to the Islamic and Christian movements to the Handsome Lake religion among the Iroquois. This provocative work is necessary reading for the student interested in a particular religious tradition, religious behavior in general, or the nature of religion in our own society.

Lewis Yablonsky. *The Hippie Trip.* New York: Pegasus, 1968.

This work is a collection of life histories of persons identifying themselves as hippies. These biographies provide the reader with a variety of personalities, backgrounds, ages, occupations, and talents.

5677

CASE STUDIES IN CULTURAL ANTHROPOLOGY

GENERAL EDITORS — George and Louise Spindler

HOLT, RINEHART AND WINSTON, INC. 383 Madison Avenue, New York 10017